WHAT

GOES

UP

A POWERFUL STORY OF REDEMPTION

WHAT

OVERCOMING
YOUR WORST

GOES

TO LIVE YOUR BEST

UP

MISTIE  LAYNE

Clovercroft Publishing

What Goes Up: Overcoming Your Worst to Live Your Best

©2019 by Mistie Layne

Published by Clovercroft Publishing, Franklin, Tennessee

Scripture taken from THE HOLY BIBLE, NEW INTERNATIONAL VERSION®, NIV® Copyright © 1973, 1978, 1984, 2011 by Biblica, Inc.™ Used by permission. All rights reserved worldwide.

Senior Editor: Tammy Kling
Executive Editor: Tiarra Tompkins
Copy Edit by Adept Content Solutions

Cover Design by Nellie Sanchez

Interior Design by Adept Content Solutions

Printed in the United States of America

978-1-948484-72-5

CONTENTS

Not only does God know our story . . . He wrote it!

—Max Lucado

A misty lane (Mistie Layne) is a foggy road which I feel perfectly reflects the path I chose to drive down . . . FOGGY. However, the warming rays from renewal of soul searching are slowly burning the fog away for this "SUNSHINE GIRL."

—Mistie Layne
AKA Daddy's "Foggy Road"
AKA Mama's "Sunshine Girl"

This book is dedicated to my three wonderful children: Lauren, Amber, and Austin. I'm sorry it took Mama so long to return home, but thank you for accepting me with open arms and unconditional love when I did. The faith and love you gave me guided me through a very volatile storm, and I know it was a rocky voyage for all of us. You are my lighthouse in a long-suffering, chaotic, and devastating storm. Thank you for believing in me and having faith God would help me conquer this. I pray you will learn from my mistakes and realize there are consequences to every decision and choice you make in life. Respect your moments of choice, they become your lifetime of decisions. Thank you to all of my family that stuck by my side and believed in me and prayed me home.

Although a life was taken, mine was saved.

ACKNOWLEDGMENTS

Dear Reader,

Each one of us will have a defining moment that alters the way we look at life forever. It may test your relationships, challenge your faith, and give you wisdom beyond your years.

What's your defining moment? Do you think it has happened yet?

This book was written eleven years ago from a small jail cell by hand on paper ordered from commissary. The pages were stained and tattered but written with passion, purpose, and humility. I thank everyone involved in any aspect of this process, as you are all a blessing to this publication. Throughout my journey I never imagined that I'd be here now, talking to you, dear reader, and sharing some of the darkest depths of my life. This is my defining moment. I want to share my scars, my heart, and my healing with the world, in hopes to help others with theirs. Your journey may not be easy, but it's worth it. Let my story guide you on yours.

I would like to acknowledge that without my faith, I might not have made it through the adversity I was confronted with. After September 18, 2007, I was consumed with guilt, remorse, and shame. However, through faith, strength is built and endurance is obtained. The Holy Spirit guided my pen to write my truth, and I hope to reach and alert others of the upcoming trauma and drama if you don't surrender your addiction, affliction, or ailments over to God or your higher power. We often ask "What does it take to hit rock bottom?" This is my story of what it took. Don't wait as long as I did. Get help, and love yourself today just as you are. Pull yourself up from any and every situation you find yourself in. Find your core strength buried inside behind the shame, guilt, embarrassment, denial, and arrogance. Get up right now and FIGHT FOR YOUR LIFE! Your life matters. Your family matters. How will you measure your dedication and commitment to yourself? Self-love begins with letting go of the things that can threaten your legacy. If you have an addiction, now is the time to focus your energy on stopping it, before it stops you. I pray that my story can change lives and shine the light on the consequences of this terrible path that so many take.

My parents loved me unconditionally and never once gave up on me. They clung to the Mistie they knew on the other side of addiction and helped pull me through all of my problems. Although I have hurt, lied, manipulated, and stolen from them, they have always been there with open arms, a true reflection of the way God loves us, His children. I am in awe.

Thank you Nona, Papa, Papa Gengo, Grandma Barbara, and my awesome kiddos Lauren, Amber, and Austin for loving me and guiding me home. This is my acknowledgment to all of you for who you are. Each one of you has helped me along the way to regain myself and who I was created to be.

MY CHILDREN ARE MY EVERYTHING.

My kids have taught me as much about life as I have tried to teach them. My individual relationships with them are each special and make my life complete. Additionally, thank you, Dorie, for the shoulder to cry on; "BC" for listening to my gumball assortment of emotions, fears, and dreams; Terri for always offering honest advice and being my best friend; Neil for showing me my strengths; and my first coach, Sam, for pushing me into what you knew I could be. I love you all. There are moments we all face in life that define us. They determine whether we will rise or fall, whether we will overcome, or shrink back from adversity.

I would like to acknowledge you, dear reader, the one who may not know me but picked up this book out of necessity, curiosity, or desperation. What is your secret pain? No matter what you're going through, you can find a way out. This is your defining moment, and I'm here for you. THERE IS HOPE!

FOREWORD

I remember the day a good friend texted to inform me that he was connecting me to someone he was certain I should meet, and someone he was equally certain possessed a story that I was going to love and relate to. In no way was I prepared for what was about to happen upon being connected to Mistie Layne; after all, what on earth could I, a fifty-six-year-old African American man with a backstory of drug addiction and incarcerations, ever have in common with a white woman who was once a Texas beauty queen?

The moment I sat down, settled in, and began reading the advance pages of *What Goes Up* provided me by my new coaching client, Mistie Layne, I was instantly swept up in a story that rivaled my own in many ways but also was far darker than anything I had ever encountered within my own darkness known as addiction. The irony of Mistie having been nearly killed herself at the age of fifteen by a person under the influence of alcohol and then experiencing all that her perpetrator had and more, well—let's just say I immediately knew it was time to buckle my seat belt. I was in for quite a ride.

What Goes Up is a book that so many of us in recovery promise ourselves that we will write one day, or wish we had the courage to dream of writing, but never do. For many in recovery it requires decades to find their way to that place that truly allows them to express each moment of their journey from entry point to exit wound. I am honored and excited that finally there is a book that speaks what so many former addicts will never be able to express, many for the simple reason that they are no lon-ger alive to express anything.

Much of what is contained within these chapters echoes the voices of all who have ever faced unbearable pain or insurmountable obstacles. For me, Mistie has peeled away many layers of the onion that I myself have, for whatever reason, been too afraid to peel for myself. For anyone who finds themselves on that quest for perfection as Mistie so candidly speaks of in her book, you will be saving yourself decades of futile searching simply by taking heed of the many life lessons shared within these pages.

I have always prided myself in being the type of individual who gives credit where credit is due, and the work that Mistie Layne has done in order to recreate and preserve a strong and viable legacy for her children and loved ones is quite remarkable.

Prepare yourself, for this story will scare you. Trust yourself, for this story will challenge you. Believe in yourself, for this story will encourage you. But most importantly, love yourself and allow this story of healing to love you in return.

Loren Michaels Harris
Motivational Speaker and
Content Creation Specialist

PREFACE

"Only 3 percent will ever make it" are the words which play over and over in my head relentlessly haunting me. The noise, smell, and bright lights are amplified and unforgiving as I wonder where I am. What has happened? I'm slowly gaining consciousness after sleeping three days straight, and bits and pieces are coming into focus. My heart is pounding, and I'm scared. Will this small, stale, cold, and depressing jail cell be my future? My lips are quivering as I peer into the plastic dull mirror because all I see is my outline, the self I used to know isn't there— am I lost in a paradox? Even though I subconsciously try to avoid it, I look down, and my eyes focus on arraignment papers, which scream "Max forty-year sentence." I'm paralyzed, I can't move, I can't even cry out loud in fear of popping into reality. . . . Oh God, is this real? My kids . . . my awesome, beautiful, and wonderful kids! Please tell me I'm having a nightmare and this isn't real life. Suddenly, I hear the loud bang as the bars to my dreary cell slam shut, and the smell of burnt fabric from the over-dried orange jump suits whips me into reality. Now I remember. . . . NO!!!! It was an accident, please, God, NO! My mind won't stop churning with "only 3 percent will make it." All I know right now is, I want to live yet feel GUILTY for being alive.

Growing up I always dreamed of the perfect soap opera life with a loving husband, kids, a big house, and a successful career. I saw life through rose-colored glasses and I wasn't prepared when reality emerged with adultery, lies, alcoholism, codependence, drug abuse, emotional, verbal and physical abuse, stress, and divorce. These influences molded my life and shaped me into exactly what and who I am today. I realize how influential those things have been in my life and have come to the realization it is time to sow healthy and productive seeds and not allow myself to be surrounded by destructive ones withered by toxic, decaying, deep-seated roots.

I grew up living a normal middle-class life with dancing lessons, sports, beauty pageants, piano lessons, big brick house with a swimming pool, my own car, and scholarships to college. I didn't want for much and admit I was rather spoiled. After twelve long years of college and allied health school, I was finally destined to fulfill my dream of becoming a surgeon. Although I was at the door of success, things changed abruptly after finding out my husband of ten years had another woman pregnant. I was devastated to find out the life I thought I was living was a lie.

After my marriage of ten years failed and ended in divorce at age thirty-one, I fell prey to depression and loneliness. Discombobulated, vulnerable, and sinking in quicksand of self-pity, I met my new best friend and lover—COCAINE. We became inseparable, spending all our time together. I soon became dependent upon it for everything. Cocaine was always there for me, day and night. I became addicted to the feeling it gave me, to the way it made everything better. Finally, I had found LOYALTY.

I'm sharing my testimony to show the devastation and havoc addiction brought to my life, my loved ones, and my friends' lives. Addiction is demanding and jealous and eventually isolates us, causing our children and family to be robbed of our time, money, and memories yet to be. I was naïve and completely blindsided by addiction, and it was out to win, *no matter what.* Please don't be misled that addiction only evolves from your neighborhood, education, color, age, sex, or upbringing. It can happen to anyone who gives it the slightest glimpse of an invitation into their life. Addiction won't stop with stripping morals, values, dignity, character, self-esteem, jobs, and bank accounts. It wants it all.

Lives were forever changed by the horrific event which occurred on the foggy, rainy unsuspecting morning of September 18, 2007. It was too late when I realized addiction doesn't just take away your judgment, but it wants to steal your soul. I didn't start my day off that morning intending for my life to take a turn, but it did.

Life instantly changed for so many with one stupid impulsive, cocaine-led decision from being in the wrong place at the wrong time with the wrong people. I have had many influences throughout my life that have driven me into decisions leading me to who I am today. Some influences landed me in a jail, while other influences helped get me home. My testimony is being shared despite embarrassment, shame, guilt, intimacy, or pride in hopes you will grasp a hold of the message and wake up to look in the mirror and start loving yourself today before more time is wasted in the darkness. My addiction has caused a great tragedy, but yours doesn't have to. Stop the madness! FORGIVE and LOVE yourself now. Throw away the cracked "toxic mirror" in which you look and peer deeper into the reflection and find your soul and true inside potential. Find something—anything—to love about yourself. Then the next day, find something else to love and embrace while slowly letting go of one negative thing at a time. Pull yourself up, one positive thought at a time.

Life hurts, and you and I both know it. Don't think for a second people in this world live a life completely free of pain, uncertainty, stress, and other trials. We all have a story to tell and some skeletons in our closets. Have you confronted yours? Have you spent time with yourself and truly looked inside to discover all that haunts you? We tend to ask, "God, why did you allow this?" or "Why me?" Please remember, the teacher is always quiet during a test. I believe my life was spared more than once so I could discover my true purpose and share my story. I believe that my life was spared to save yours.

I invite you into my heart and mind as I describe to you a wild ride through my crazy rollercoaster life. I want this to be more than another typical story of adversity, I want to offer HOPE and share what I did to dig myself out of a hopeless situation. Don't wait; start now by making lifelong changes. Learn to love yourself, with your flaws, and surrender the pain. Replace sadness, loneliness, and resentments with peace, joy, faith, and self-confidence. Each small choice we make every hour in every day can alter our course. Choose wisely. The influences that drive us can determine our future. Are you driving under positive or destructive influences? Are you surrounded by people that will build you up or bring you down? Take a serious look at your environment, and remember we are the sum of the five closest people we hang with.

Take a step to make a change because there is one guarantee in life: YOU WILL DIE. The real question is, how do you want to exit this world? What legacy would you be leaving behind? What would your tombstone say, and would anyone show up for your funeral? How would your obituary sound, and who would write it? Ponder these things in quiet time with yourself, dig deep honestly, and face your reality. This is my story of what it took— the real, raw, unedited version of me and what it took for me to climb up from my rock bottom.

Please know that if you feel you are at your rock bottom, you can get out too. Have faith. First, stop blaming others. God doesn't tempt us to do evil but will send trials to test our faith (James 1:13). Those trials build pressure deep down inside where we often try and hide sin, shameful habits, and neglect. In searching for inner peace, we must admit, confront, and repent of those pains openly and honestly. Denial is only effective for short-term pain management by shielding us of traumatic situations. However, as denial melts away, the truth emerges, and we are forced to face our inner fears, pains, and shame. Rather than numbing these feelings with cocaine, I've learned to go face to face and challenge each one to discover what life lesson was intended by it. My sister Terri reminds me, "Everything is going wrong just right because God is in control." Therefore, when Satan tries to use bad memories, bad habits, or shameful events to bring me down, I stop and ask myself, "If my kids know God through the things they see in me, what would God look like to them?" Would they draw a mommy passed out on the couch after returning from a four-day drug mission or daddy always drunk? Would they illustrate the fighting, arguing, and violence? Does it stop you in your tracks and make you think? Imagine them drawing your picture—how would you look? How would your family unit look on a Crayola picture posted in a second-grade classroom? Get honest and do a reality check. I was shocked when I finally came to terms with my TRUTH.

Proverbs 4:23   Guard your heart, for it is the wellspring from which all life flows.

CHAPTER ONE

ROOTS RUN DEEP

The dress was bright yellow with large white polka dots, ruffles, and a sash accessorized with black patent leather shoes, lacy socks, and long white gloves. I'll never forget what I wore the day I won my first beauty pageant at age four and crowned "Miss Tiny Tot Review." The feeling of pride and specialness overtook my emotions as I prissed up to receive my crown. I learned at an early age the POWER that comes with winning. I thrived on that power for years in pageants, tap, jazz, ballet, toe, twirling, basketball, piano, and clarinet, all of which were the building blocks of my competitiveness for many years to come. I constantly found myself seeking other people's approval and praise. I put undue stress on myself to be perfect and the best at everything I did. I set high goals with a mad passion to become a surgeon and knew from a very early age I wanted to achieve greatness and had the determination to do whatever it took to get there. I had always dreamt of being a princess and living happily ever after with my Prince Charming living the fairytale life. I was determined to reach my dreams.

Do you remember your childhood dreams? What stood in your way? Did you lack the confidence to go after those dreams? Is it too late to go after them now? Honestly, is it *really* too late?

1

My momma (Nona) dedicated her life to my brother Damon and me, and growing up I admired her and thought her to be the most beautiful and classy lady I'd ever seen. She carried herself with pride and dignity and just seemed so "perfect." She was a true Italian woman of beauty, sophistication, and style.

She had rheumatic fever as a child and spent many years bedridden and didn't have a normal childhood, so she always tried making all that up by giving me every opportunity in life she never had. After she delivered Damon in 1961, the doctors advised she wait a few years before becoming pregnant again so her heart could regain strength. She feared she would only be allowed the birth of one more child and prayed for a little girl. Six years later her treasured "Sunshine Girl" arrived in a small humid south-east Texas town in August 1967, and she has loved me unconditionally since.

She always had me well-groomed and immaculately dressed when I was growing up. I competed in pageants and learned very young the emphasis society puts on beauty. I liked being all made up fancy and pretty, but I wanted to be a normal country kid and get dirty too. My Aunt Coco and Grandma Blondie would pick me up to go play with my cousins and strip me down to my panties to run around in mud puddles, run through the woods barefoot, and get as dirty as I could. I remember the smell of pine needles and how the sticky humidity put my already curly hair in tight little ringlets. Before my mom would arrive to pick me up, they would have me clean and all pieced back together again. I thrived on the DECEPTION at an early age of "getting away" with something, later realizing how deception was a tool the enemy used, and provided fuel for my fire.

I remember running the neighborhood with Tami, Sissy, T-Joe and Jeffery and mom saying she could always spot me coming down the road as the leader of the pack. I constantly pushed the limits and always convinced them to join me in my mischief. We spent hours making huts in the woods, playing in the tree house, and picking berries. Those were fun times of innocence. Simple times back then.

I went to school in a small town of about 12,000 and realize how fortunate I was to grow up with the same kids year after year and never have to change schools. I was truly a spoiled brat, and my parents were particularly protective. It appeared we had it all—we were the perfect family. I was naïve to the abnormalities or hardships most people call the hard knocks of life. I had lived a sheltered life, and my outlook on everything was positive, as a kid's life should be. However, once I grew up I wasn't at all prepared to deal with real life.

I started out a pre-med major at Lamar University on scholarship for baton twirling and clarinet. I had a one-track path of achieving my dream of going to medical school. My life seemed so perfect, so innocent, and untainted, and I thought I was on easy street. However, I was living a life of facades, cover-ups, denials, and pressures to be perfect and successful. Apparently, things weren't as perfect as I thought. Later in life while writing my life story in rehab, hidden dark secrets about my childhood surfaced. Those memories were shoved deep under layers of denial or self-preservation or a combination of both over the years. Funny how we are able to suppress and play "pretend" even as adults for self-preservation in fear our dark secrets will emerge from our memory banks. I am going to take you through my journey with raw truth knowing that some will judge me and others will cry.

I have spent years desperately trying to cover the secrets about my life, but have now embraced my past and will shout my RAW TRUTH without further hesitation. There will be no sugar coating the scenes of my one–person play. EVERY event in my life has shaped me, and I'm not ashamed, just disappointed in choices I've made along the way. If my truth can release someone else's denial, then it will all be worth it, even if it only touches and changes one person's life. The shame of my past has kept me a slave to depression, feelings of inadequacy, and low self-esteem, and I don't want that to happen to you.

Deciding to release my truth to help others is the silver lining and how I cope with the incredibly harmful and shameful things I've done. In order to pull myself up, I had to EMBRACE my past and quit being ashamed and feeling guilty, and I had to use it in a positive light to help others.

Growing up under the shadow of my brother Damon was tough as he succeeded at everything. Damon was the star in local- and state-level plays and was a hard act to follow, literally. He was smart, clever, charming, talented, popular, witty, and always a star in the spotlight. I was constantly striving to be as "perfect" as I saw him in my eyes. Following in school six years behind, I was expected by his teachers to excel as he did. Predestined expectations from teachers, band directors, parents, and family promoted me being self-driven, self-motivated, and self-demanding. Fortunately, I was able to meet most of their expectations but thought I worked harder than he ever appeared to. However, I soon became a very overwhelmed overachiever, and little did I know the influence of PERFECTIONISM would drive me and be a force to reckon with. I'm my own worst enemy and criticize and ridicule myself far better than anyone else ever can. I give myself a brutal beating in my head about any subpar performance or task.

Due to the age difference, Damon and I argued a lot as I was the pesky little sister, but there is also a closeness we have always shared. I remember how gentle he was with me in third grade when I asked to change my name to "Pink Flower." Laughing, he explained that I couldn't change my name but that he would call me that the rest of his life. To this day, my kids often address letters and cards to me as Pink Flower, and it is refreshing because during some of my darkest times, I felt more like a black rose. Another silver lining in pulling myself up and not focusing on the negative is recognizing a rose is beautiful, regardless of the color, and I accepted my rose as a positive attribute, even with the flaws and prickly thorns.

My dad, Ken (Papa Gengo), was a workaholic and brilliant entrepreneur owning an air condition business and Mexican restaurant. He always had many irons in the fire, and my mom hated his long hours. Although his hard work instilled a great work ethic in me, I later resented his time away. As Momma served dinner, Daddy would pull into the driveway, and we joked he must have smelled the food and came home right in time to eat. He was a great provider for the family and worked very hard but was absent quite a bit in my younger years.

I remember proudly prancing around in my daddy's tool belt and trying so hard to be rough and tough to assist him with his work. He thought it was cute that I called the Phillips screwdriver a "Plus" and a flathead a

"Minus" (still do). I thought I was really something when he taught me to tape and float sheetrock, tar a roof, and lay rebar while building our house. I have a scar on my left hand from the rebar ripping through my hand, and he nearly lost his finger erecting that house by cutting it with a skill saw. Our old home holds beautiful memories for me of swimming pool parties, big family gatherings, and happy times. When my dad was home, he was always playing the piano or guitar and singing, and I get goose bumps when a familiar song plays that reminds me of him.

Daddy was previously married, and I have a half-brother and half-sister, Kenny and Therese. What is this "half" stuff anyway? A brother is a brother and a sister is a sister; at least that's what I was taught. They are ten and twelve years older and lived in California, so we weren't very close as kids. However, later in life as we grew up, we had more in common and built life-long bonds. Sadly, some relationships were tarnished by drama, trauma, and strife in our family, and I really miss the closeness we all once had. Ironically, Kenny is closer to my ex-husband, Eric, than he is to me. While sitting in my jail cell, they were on a cruise together, and I must admit that hurt because he's *my* brother! Seriously, back then I only saw my ex-husband as an adulterer, alcoholic, and deadbeat who never paid me one penny of child support. Through healing and forgiveness, I see things differently now, but back then felt betrayed because Kenny is *my* brother. To this day, they are very close, and although it is strange, I no longer resent it because I embrace my actions and accountability. I am not the "people pleaser" I once tried to be, and as you continue to read, you will realize I was far from perfect and had my share of the blame in all of this.

My sister, Therese (Terri), is a role model to me because she is strong in her faith and very forgiving and loving. She has always given me the benefit of the doubt and accepted me as I am. Without her love, support, and determination, I might not have found my way back. I have so much respect for her as a mother, sister, and sister in Christ. She lives on the West Coast, and we don't visit like we should, but we have a healthy relationship and will always be there for each other. I love and miss you, Sis!

I'm the caboose of a middle-class family, the apple of my daddy's eye and my mother's treasured "Sunshine Girl." I constantly tried to gain their approval and attention and felt I was expected to succeed and achieve everything I aimed to. I sometimes felt inadequate because my older siblings would engage in intelligent conversations of politics, religion, and economics with my father. Of course, I was younger and didn't take part in their "grown up" conversations, so felt left out. I was used to being in the spotlight and felt shunned. Why did I feel "less" than them? I was driven constantly to be perfect, and when I wasn't, I internalized all the letdowns of failure. My dad was also a chemist like me, and we shared other traits as well, such as being go-getters and multi-taskers, fast talking our way out of anything, and being movers and shakers. But when it came to logical everyday life, I was green and naïve and had little to no common sense. Sometimes I would tell myself I was the outcast and felt inadequate among my family. This was just ridiculous. Why would I put that pressure on myself at such an early age? Who was I trying to impress or please as a little girl?

CHAPTER TWO

LIFE HAPPENS

Mom hovered over me as the rain from her umbrella dripped on my face. Why was I lying on the cold wet ground?

It took moments before I remembered. There were headlights coming at us from the left driver's side, and then everything slowed down as my brain calculated and finally realized that there was no way we were avoiding the collision.

God, I'm having a very hard time breathing now. Where is Roger? My thoughts reeled in a sea of confusion. When I look back at that memory, some of it is a blur but other parts are crystal clear. I remember thinking, *Oh good, he's sitting on the back of an ambulance and seems to be okay.* I remember the pain and thinking clearly about it.

I had sharp stabbing pains with every breath I took, and my face felt cold. The night was dark, and I was tired and weak. The paramedics put harnesses around my neck and wrapped my entire body as they dug the ground from beneath me. I was scared!

Am I dying? I wondered.

Mom sobbed uncontrollably, and my father was frantic, trying to make sure nobody was moving me too fast. I remember thinking, *Okay, I get it now; I'm either about to die or hurt pretty badly.*

My car was hit by a drunk driver two blocks from my house. It was my sophomore year of high school. Apparently, God wasn't ready for me because I lived after being told the passenger seat where I sat had been completely crushed. My life was spared, but at fifteen I didn't realize the value in that. Surrounded by the love, the concern of my parents, and the fragility of life—you would've thought I would learn to value life, but I didn't learn. Some people never learn until it's too late.

At the hospital my life teetered back and forth for several hours, and my parents were put through the agony of not knowing if I'd live or die. I had broken two ribs and slammed my face through the windshield and needed plastic surgery on my eye. Although mom and dad were scared beyond imagination as I lay in the hospital recovering, they were grateful I wasn't hurt worse. Looking back now, I can see how loving and grateful they were and how my later experiences, choices, actions, and drug-related vanishing acts would be far more agonizing for them. I realize in hindsight, God had a plan for me to do something special with my life. He saved me for a reason.

Today I look back and think; how pitiful, because I'm sure His plan wasn't for me to become a drug addict and waste ten precious years of the life already graciously spared. I can see the reality and still understand that I've gotten yet another chance.

I grew like any other child and recovered, going back to school. I graduated, and I imagine that moment was far more special than anyone ever thought it would be.

I was excited as I packed my bags for a Texas A&M scholarship college tour the next morning, then it came out of nowhere. "We are going to stay at Aunt Sandy's for a while." My heart was pounding and I started to fear her next words: "Your dad and I are separating."

There it was, the words I had been fearing to hear my entire junior year. I knew there were problems and had started recognizing the tension in our "not so perfect" home. I felt overwhelmed with emotion and confused about how to react. My stomach knotted.

"Okay," I said.

Almost immediately I began having a battle in my head of who to choose. Nobody asked me to choose, but I knew it was coming . . .

Mom or Dad? How would I make that decision without feeling as if I've let one of them down and hurt their feelings? I put so much pressure on myself.

Panic set in, and as a teenager I began internalizing all of the pressure and feeling sorry for myself. After all, what will happen to *me*? The thoughts reeled in my head. Will I still get to live in our big brick house with the swimming pool? Will I still get to go to college?

That night at my aunt's house, my mind raced with all the questions about where I would end up and how my senior year would be affected by THEIR divorce.

I awoke to the telephone ringing, but wasn't really paying attention as I was so concerned about myself and how *their* traumatic divorce was going to ruin *my* life. Suddenly I heard a commotion and realized mom was hysterical.

Oh my God, what was happening now?

My Aunt Sandy walked into the room and calmly sat down. "Honey, your dad is in the hospital. There has been a bad fire in your house, and he was trapped inside."

We raced to the hospital, and as I walked towards his room the fear of how he would look consumed me. I imagined him unrecognizable and how I would feel about his disfigurement. My neighbor had seen the fire and responded quickly by pulling him out of the house, but I was scared he had been burned head to toe. He had pulled my dad out and saved him. He wasn't burnt beyond recognition, but he did have significant lung damage. He was going to live—and to me that's all that mattered—my dad was going to live.

Later that night we pulled up to the house to witness the aftermath, and the air smelled like a bonfire with tiny particles dancing and floating in the slight breeze. After a house fire, the scent of it remains in the air and travels throughout the neighborhood for days and often weeks. I walked in hesitantly to survey the damage. The kitchen was melted beyond recognition, and all I could do was cry, and run straight to my room to check for anything left.

My mother and I were in shock.

I noticed my homecoming corsages were not burnt, but so much other stuff was destroyed and melted. Mom sobbed uncontrollably, holding the little flower pot I made her in second grade and the pot holders I had loomed. "They survived!" she said through tears, smiling.

She made me realize materialistic things are replaceable, but family heirlooms and lives are not. In a moment I realized how quickly life could change. One moment life could be normal, and then suddenly it could drastically change. Each of these experiences impacted our family in a powerful way and throughout it all, the love for and from my parents never wavered.

So how did I end up an addict? Looking back I can see that it was completely my choice. I've had plenty of time to trace the path of my life and my errors, to see the ways in which life changed me. It was a slow fade, a gradual occurrence, and choice after bad choice slowly led me into the darkness.

Growing up I was known as a "good girl," never going on the "wrong side of the tracks." I didn't drink, smoke, or do drugs. I rarely cussed and demanded respect from others back then but later allowed men to emotionally, verbally, and physically abuse me. This is how the path to addiction changes you. This is how the road to needing a drug morphs an individual into something they are not. What happened?

How did I get there from being a CONFIDENT and STRONG student, from a middle class family from the country? As a teen I always allowed influences of perfectionism to drive me to be extremely competitive and got consumed by guilt and shame when I failed. Of course, all of this pressure was self-induced, and I was exhausted by trying to dominate things to ensure they went "my" way. I found myself often saying "Wouldn't it be better this way?" or "Let me handle it." Of course, by "handling it" I would ensure it would be done right, or *my way*. Additionally, I internalized every situation, casting blame on myself for things happening around me. If only my parents didn't have arguments over me, maybe they wouldn't divorce. If I hadn't had an earlier curfew than the other passengers in the car, our wreck would have never happened. I tended to end up disillusioned or aggravated most of the time, letting any little glitch rule my happiness, mood, or success. I made sure to overwhelm myself to stay busy by volunteering at everything, joining several clubs, and constantly putting on a show of immense strength to impress others. Maybe it was ego and not a desire to be perfect, but a desire to seem as if I was. I always cared about the opinions of others, and I would do anything to make sure I didn't have to say no or let them down.

It has been suggested that the root of perfectionism is poor self-esteem and people-pleasing. I believe a beautiful person can be ugly on the inside and vice versa, and that a person intent on pleasing others will ultimately lose themselves.

When my own children arrived I carried that desire for achievement into my parenting. I loved them with all my heart. I now strive for inner beauty and happiness and no longer use my performances as a meter of praise and attention, but as a new mom I had a lot to learn and made several mistakes. My daughter Amber is very similar to me in that she is driven, motivated, and puts tremendous emphasis on performance in academics and sports. I tried to praise and reward her involvement rather than the accomplishments and achievements but somehow failed at that too and bragged as any parent would. I have been accused of putting Amber on a pedestal and causing resentment from Lauren and Austin. They say Amber is my favorite! I have no favorite. I only boasted about her many accomplishments and didn't realize what effect this had on the others. I was never a perfect mom, even before my addictions, but they knew they were loved and that we had a happy family.

Parenting is exhausting and challenging. We put undue pressure on ourselves trying to keep up with the Joneses and risk self-destruction. Is drug addiction generational, spiritually connected, or passed down? My parents never did drugs. I taught my kids not to do drugs. Yet I ended up on drugs.

My children have witnessed firsthand the wake of destruction that drug abuse causes. I cling daily to Psalm 103 because God makes a promise to heal us of our addictions, afflictions, and ailments. My attitude now toward drugs is "been there, done that," and I hope my children take a stand rather than fall prey to drugs providing a temporary and false sense that everything will be okay. There is so much exposure and peer pressure in our schools today to try drugs, from ecstasy, heroin, K2, bath salts, marijuana, cocaine, crystal meth, pills, and alcohol. I pray my addiction caused enough havoc in their lives to sway their choices.

When I began using drugs, it surprised everyone. I would hear "Oh no! Not Mistie." Hearing that only fueled my anger because I thought, *Why NOT Mistie?* Didn't they all realize I was just a normal human being? The pressure of being on a pedestal became so overwhelming; sometimes I WANTED to be bad!

My mom was floored to learn I had turned to drugs at age thirty-one, my first year entering medical school. She always said she could have dealt with it better if I had experimented as a teenager when it is almost expected instead of waiting until I was a mother of two. As previously warned, addiction can take hold of anyone at any age at any time in their life. Stay alert regarding your choices.

What's my message in this book? Not to be flowery, or win a literary award or to be on stages. It is my simple desire to save lives by providing HOPE when all seems HOPELESS. My message is that even trying drugs once is the worst decision you can make. Set boundaries. Choose your time wisely. TICK TOCK!

Beware! Addiction is no joke. My parents had been strict, and fair, but as a teen I didn't think of it as fair. Looking back I remember that when I turned sixteen late in summer before my junior year, my parents wouldn't let me date a boy alone. Although at the time I thought my life would end and my parents were too strict, I now understand why. Therefore, both of my daughters had to wait until sixteen to date too. I find it funny that we mimic parenting styles we once complained of because that is the only exposure we know, or we have come to realize they were right.

When my daughter Amber turned sixteen, it was two months before I landed in jail facing a forty-year sentence. Needless to say, I missed her first date, many of Lauren's cheerleading competitions, their proms, doctor appointments, the day they started their periods, Austin's first steps, his first day of kindergarten, and so much more during my ten-year hiatus from real life. People that know me are probably questioning how I could ever allow all this to happen because I am super involved in their lives now. Well, the truth is I didn't let it happen—addiction took over my life, and I felt too weak and too enslaved to fight it. I even missed both of my girls' high school graduations. I felt hopeless against the battle and any chance of forgiveness.

My high school days were some of my fondest, happiest carefree days, and I regret that now my girls are left with memories of their mother only being around some of the time and "missing" the rest. How insecure I must have made them feel! There are no second chances to re-create those memories. Remember that. If there is one thing you take from this book today please remember that *time* is not a healer—*it's a thief!* If you aren't paying attention, time will rob you blind. My kids had lost their mother. It was as if I had died. Their memories of those important events will never change.

Can I stop for a moment and address you, dear reader?

Maybe you have no issues with addiction at all. Maybe you're just in need of a reminder to be more present. Or maybe you're hiding something from everyone. Maybe you drink too much. Maybe you use pills. Maybe it's something illegal. STOP! I want so badly for you to pull yourself up right now and not have to endure these painful memories that live within me and my kids forever. It's your choice. Choose to be clear minded and let go of the toxic things that you're using to numb the pain. If you are already enslaved to an addiction, seek help and don't give up until you succeed. YOU are worth fighting for.

Again, how did I allow all this? I often look in the mirror and question who I see and wonder who I was back then. God uses every situation for the good because these trials and tribulations have given me the passion to fight addiction, domestic abuse, and self-pity. The day it all changed for me, I found myself looking into that toxic mirror with two choices staring me in the face: either succumb to the addiction or PULL MYSELF UP!!! Strength came out of nowhere the day I *decided* to live.

Some must be thinking, "This is just a spoiled rich white girl looking for attention." You might ask, "What the hell is her problem?" Well, I'm figuring it all out, but something was definitely wrong even before my drug addiction, or I wouldn't have started pulling my eyelashes out until they were all gone my senior year of high school. Was this an internal rebellion against perfectionism and beauty pageants? Why was I self-destructing when it seemed I had everything going for me? Those problems then barely even contend with what I've chosen to endure later in life. I thought I was a perfectly normal child from a normal family.

CHAPTER THREE

CODEPENDENCY AND DISAPPOINTMENT

Eric was a good-looking, talented, cocky, arrogant, smart-ass Cajun who I met my freshman year in college. We fell in love and had so much fun together marching in the band and pursuing our degrees. He played trombone, and I played clarinet and twirled batons on scholarship. My parents had recently divorced and instead of bouncing back and forth between them, I spent all my time with Eric. He was different than other guys I had chosen to date before. He was rude, arrogant, and cocky, but in the most charming way. He introduced me to a more normal and typical life of cussing, drinking, and real-life happening front and center instead of all the pretending and secrets I had discovered my family was made of. Maybe all college students experience this freedom and adventure for the first time, but it was more than that–he was my escape.

We continued dating and living the famed college life of fraternity parties and being young and carefree trying to mature into responsible adults. I was a pre-med major, and he studied music, and things progressed as we dated, and before I knew it, he asked me to marry him. I said yes and planned a wedding in the Catholic Church.

I had been going to mass with my mom, but my dad would not attend with us due to his own personal reasons. I don't remember my dad ever being in church except when I made my First Communion. It wasn't until my late thirties when I sat beside my Dad in a church and worshiped God for the first time. I am thankful he was saved, and later he and his new wife Barbara turned out to be the strongest Christian influences in my life.

Although I was on birth control pills, I became pregnant with our first child, Lauren. Because I became pregnant before my actual wedding date, the priest would no longer allow us to marry in the church. I couldn't believe it, my world of dreams was crashing down! My plans changed, and we were married by a Justice of the Peace, and although the court room was packed with loved ones, my marriage ceremony was a BIG disappointment. Like most little girls, I dreamed of a large beautiful fairy tale wedding with all the fuss. I was so crushed not to have my big dress, my dad walking me down the aisle, and the consecration of marriage being performed in God's house. More disappointments emerged as our honeymoon plans were mixed up and we spent the night in the wrong city. Eric was mad and full of Budweiser, so we didn't even sleep together that night. I was so devastated–everything was going wrong, except for my beautiful Lauren growing in my womb.

As newlyweds, we stumbled into life together. Eric spent an intimate night with Budweiser, and I was alone. Budweiser was part of our family too; not just on weekends or at fraternity party's anymore, but it became an everyday member of the family as Eric's mistress. I assumed he drank to numb the pain and responsibility of fatherhood so early. Another huge disappointment! We brought a beautiful big blue eyed precious little girl into the world together, and that was my new purpose, my new happiness. Lauren watched every romantic Disney movie and dreamt big like I had as a little girl, in love with the notion of being in love. Her love of "love" was innocent, hopeful and refreshing. I started wondering if I was in love with Eric, or just in love with love too.

Looking back of course, I wish I could have given her the perfect childhood, but I didn't. However, today I can see that the silver lining from the storm she was forced to live through is that she has become literally the strongest woman I know and is a SUPERHERO with how she cares for and loves her daughters. She is beautiful, smart, talented, whimsical, and full of compassion.

For the next ten years, my mood was dependent on how Eric woke up that day. He was a master manipulator, and when he was mad could give me the silent treatment for days at a time. I would cook a nice meal, and he would punish ME by not eating; games, manipulation, and cruelty. I found myself relying on HIS good moods for MY happiness and using the bad days to form my own relationship with Little Debbie and her very fattening snack cakes to make me happy. I was empty, lonely, and searching for acceptance. I felt if he only loved me more, then he would quit drinking. I convinced myself it was somehow *my* fault, again internalizing the failure.

Eventually, Eric quit college and went to work in the refineries as a boilermaker, bringing home very good money. I worked during the day for my stepdad as an office manager and went to school faithfully at night to keep my dream of becoming a surgeon alive. I worked, went to school, and took care of Lauren but became lonely and overwhelmed because Eric worked out of state three weeks at a time, and I basically felt like a single parent.

Depression was setting in, and I continued relying on food for comfort. Eric hounded me when I gained weight yet cut up my miniskirt and complained when other men gave me too much attention. He made me give up teaching tap dance at night, so I was no longer dancing and slowly started gaining weight while trying to find happiness at the bottom of a McDonald's French fry box. I had placed as a runner-up in the Miss Texas Teen Bluebonnet beauty pageant just two years before, but then after I had a baby, I gained twenty pounds. Of course, that was nowhere near obesity at 135 pounds, but I felt I could never please him and started losing my self-esteem when I didn't have his approval. I was becoming reclusive and miserable because instead of being happy with myself, I was depending on others to validate me and make me happy. This wasn't the soap opera marriage I had envisioned; what happened? What had I done wrong? How did I fail? This must be *my* fault!

Have you ever been in a situation where you blame yourself for oth-ers' bad choices or behaviors? If so, my friends, we are what people call "enablers." I had to learn how to stop enabling my alcoholic husband so I attended Al-Anon meetings to learn to break my codependency. Old habits and emotional abuse were wedged stubbornly within making it hard to stand up against the norm; therefore I failed miserably at this too.

We were living in Austin, Texas, away from our family so I could attend the University of Texas (UT). Two-and-one-half years later, I became pregnant with our second daughter, Amber. Since Eric worked out of town and wasn't home with me, I would beg him to move to Albuquerque where I could enlist help from my mom, but he always said "NO." I would hang up, stewing with resentment inside, and say "ass-hole" aloud. I wasn't aware Lauren was always listening and at three years old was like a little tape recorder. One day when I'd had enough, I hung up and said "Lauren, we are moving to Albuquerque to be with Nona and Papa." She lit up like a Christmas tree and said, "Daddy's not an asshole anymore?" WOW! Another reality check: our kids are smart, perceptive, and very intuitive. They are always listening and paying attention to our body language, movements, moods, and words.

Tired of being alone and now pregnant, I called my brother Damon to come help us pack up and take us to Albuquerque, New Mexico, where my mom relocated with her new husband Bill (Papa.) I needed their sup-port because I was trying to keep my dream alive by staying in college. I had to work, raise Lauren, be a daughter, a wife, and now go through a pregnancy basically alone as Eric was out of town for work. I rented a cute three-bedroom brick house in the back of a cul-de-sac, and that was our home for the next seven years. It seemed good and normal then. The girls both learned to ride their bikes there, which is probably the only "normal" childhood memory they each have with me.

A neighbor boy named Marcus was Lauren's best friend, and his mother named her little girl Lorena (after Lauren). Mr. Pearl was the neighborhood grandpa and loved our girls very much. Hours were spent sitting under Mr. Pearl's shade tree talking and watching the girls run around the cul-de-sac. He taught them to wink, and when they did, he gave them a fresh cut rose from his yard. We loved him and the normalcy his memory brought us. Lauren and Amber both visited him on recent trips to Albuquerque, but he passed away before I could make it there to let him know I was back to the person he mentored before the cocaine took over my life. I miss those years and all the memories of camping, taking ski trips to Purgatory, soccer practice, open house at school, PTA meetings, Christmas and Thanksgiving gatherings, and daily family life. We were a family: me, Eric, Lauren, Amber, and Budweiser. How did it all go astray? It was a series of small moments, not one big wrong decision.

One afternoon I was washing Eric's clothes after he returned home from work in California and found a frequently called number on his hotel bill. Being the straightforward, aggressive Leo I am, I called the number and found out something that altered my course in life. Eric had gotten another woman pregnant, and she claimed to have had a miscarriage on Christmas Eve. My life was devastated because the specialness of being privileged to be the only woman to carry Eric's child was now tarnished by another woman's womb. I speculate there could be other children because not only did he sleep with her, but her sister too. Apparently, he was frequenting strip clubs and having a ball while I was home raising his two kids, going to school, and working full time. Why was he doing this? What was wrong with me? I was always told I was pretty and smart and considered myself a good wife and mother. I was a very involved mother and was a "Super Mom" in PTA, room mother, soccer mom, and church volunteer. The girls were in ice skating and soccer, and we seemed happy enough. I was definitely an overachiever and over-doer, and I became overwhelmed. My mom used to tell me if I didn't slow down, I would end up a "runaway" mom. HOW did she predict my future? I would have never even considered doing any drugs at that time in my life and had often turned them down at parties many times in the past.

Apparently, adultery became a permanent fixture in my life because most men I've been with have managed to thrust that knife deeper into my heart as I cried tears of inadequacy, thinking something was wrong with me. I retaliated and fought fire with fire and pain with pain. While Eric was away working, I found myself involved with a college friend that gave me attention and realized my marriage was rocky and not as good as I led others to believe. We attended marriage counseling, and Eric quit his job after I demanded he quit traveling. He enrolled back in college, and we were making an honest effort to save our marriage. We went on a seven-day cruise to the Western Caribbean to spend time alone and work things out, but I sadly realized our marriage was over when all he did was drink beer by the pool, stare at women, and make me feel inadequate (I later learned, I allowed him to make me feel this way). Oh, did I mention, Budweiser came on board too?

Suddenly, I realized how naïve and blind I had been and tried to fool myself by avoiding the problems we were having. Later, I also found out the night before we married he slept with two women. Meanwhile my mom and I were in a hotel room with me throwing up and nauseated from being pregnant. How could my life have been such a lie and I not know? I loved this man and gave him 100 percent of my heart and thought that was enough. I was wrong! Real life problems blindsided me, and I was not prepared for any of it.

The divorce came after Eric was charged with sexual harassment at work, and I found out about another affair with a blonde haired, blue eyed girl named Michelle (Bimbo #1). After our separation, I went to his apartment early one morning to drop the girls off because he didn't show up to get them so I could do my 6:00 a.m. pharmacy rotation at school. The door was open at his apartment, so when he didn't answer after knocking, I went in. I found him and Bimbo #1 naked in the bed. The Bimbo ran and hid like a punk-ass bitch in the bathroom and locked the door. I reacted by swinging and cracking Eric's jaw with one punch! Am I now abusive or just a lady scorned? Ten years of lies, emotional and verbal abuse, and his affair with Budweiser was built up and released in one swing. All I could do was ball up my fist and let all the pain and anger out. Memories of the drinking, porn, cheating, calling me names, and silent treatments were in my head. I remember a previous argument when Eric left and I looked down into Lauren's big blue eyes and said, "Never let a man talk to you like that." She responded, "Then why do *you* let Daddy?" That opened my eyes how I was teaching her to do as I say, not as I do.

I now realized my marriage was over, and I just wanted out. However, I was unaware how others around us would be affected by our divorce too. Times were getting rough emotionally, and the night Eric and his newly pregnant Bimbo #1 drove away from our cul-de-sac in a U-Haul van, Lauren chased him down the street crying. She was eight and Amber was five, and that was one of the hardest nights of my life as I lay with both of them sobbing for their daddy.

Lauren asked why he was leaving us, and I tried to explain he needed to move to Texas to be near his mamma (Nanny). She said, "I guess Daddy loves Nanny more than us." What was I supposed to say to that? My heart was broken for them and for myself, and I spent the next several months rocking them both to sleep as they cried for their daddy night after night. He was a very interactive father and played with them and they missed him terribly. Although this seemed so hard on them, later in life I did so much more damage to them by being a part-time mommy and those precious little angels have cried so many more tears. If only I could go back and make better choices; "If only, should have, could have, would have." We can't dwell on those words because they will only bring us down.

Our divorce started a ripple effect of heartaches, and I wondered, *Was it all my fault?* I must have been the reason Eric cheated and left us, right? I convinced myself something must have been wrong with me, and I started doubting my self-worth, intelligence, beauty, sexuality, and self-esteem. I often found myself looking lost in the mirror asking, "Who are you?" This was the beginning of the end of sweet innocent Mistie Layne, the "good" girl everyone loved, protected, and respected. It all changed in a flash, and I'm awestruck how quickly Satan took control and ownership of my life after giving him the slightest open door. When we give in to Satan's lies, we open the door of destruction. I went from an energetic, young, beautiful, carefree, inspiring woman with ambitions of becoming a surgeon to sitting behind bars facing forty years. How did I arrive at this juncture? *God, please forgive me!*

CHAPTER FOUR

DEPRESSION

Sometimes the hardest moments hit you like an unexpected tidal wave until you think you're going to drown. Anger can't erase or replace hurt, but it provides a temporary platform to overcome the loss that you feel. Oftentimes, anger manifests into depression or even invokes physical abuse. It is important we deal with anger and not let it harden our heart.

When Eric left, he cleared our bank account and left me and the girls financially broke and broken hearted. Of course, like most alcoholic fathers that abandon their children, he never paid the $32,000 child support he was court ordered to pay. I was angry for many years and harbored resentment for him breaking up our family with his affairs, drinking and leaving the state. I blamed him for everything! This is the "stinkin'-thinkin'" that sets in: I thought my drug addiction was his fault because if he hadn't cheated, we wouldn't be divorced, and I would have never fallen victim to cocaine. I eventually learned to take my own culpability in every situation, embrace it, and move forward. Although I was angry with him, I began fixating on my flaws, convincing myself I must have caused him to cheat. Picking myself apart and assuming I was to blame only set the tempo for me internalizing future failures.

Even though we are making mistakes while forging ahead, it is still called progress. I eventually became thankful Eric was physically there for our girls when I later abandoned them. Although he was the cause for our family breaking up, I have done far greater damage with the turn I allowed my life to take.

Leading up to the divorce I was accepted into the Nuclear Medicine program which I found interesting with my Chemistry background. I tackled school full time while putting in 2,000 clinical hours, working thirty-six hours on the weekends doing telemetry in the hospital, and now raising my two girls alone as my marriage was dissolving in front of my eyes. The divorce left me stressed, lonely, and isolated, and I wasn't in a very good place mentally. Soon after I graduated the Nuclear Medicine program I was accepted into medical school. I was at the gate of my dreams but depression was setting in and I became extremely overwhelmed when Eric moved to Texas. Nona and Papa picked up the slack financially and gave me relief with babysitting. Any visits the girls made to Eric in Texas, I pushed and paid for. The girls missed him so much and I thought it would be good for them to see him, even though he had made little to no effort to see them. Apparently he and Bimbo #1 were too busy starting his *new* family 1100 miles away.

When I first became pregnant with Lauren at age twenty, my Dad was concerned I wouldn't finish my education. He told me I'd just ruined my future, and he was extremely disappointed in me. His negativity and lack of faith alone kept me driven—thank you for making me dead set on proving you wrong, Daddy! After years of staying in school a few classes at a time, my dad and stepmom (Grandma Barbara) sent me an index card that read, "Keep plugging away, Baby, and one day you will get where you are going." That card remained on my refrigerator door until my twelfth year of college when I finally earned a BS in psychology and chemistry and a degree in nuclear medicine. I did it! Well, of course—I'm an overachiever, remember. I beat the odds. I succeeded, regardless of the forces pushing against me. I never gave up. Do you feel you are up against a wall that seems too high to ever hurdle? I promise, if you just take one step after another, eventually you will get to your destination. The key is to NEVER GIVE UP and always BELIEVE IN YOURSELF, even if others don't.

I landed an awesome job in nuclear medicine and was making great money but was becoming more and more depressed. I started drowning my emotional pain with "Little Debbie" again. I had become a true addict . . . of Zebra Cakes! Wouldn't that be so simple and cheap compared to cocaine? As you will learn in upcoming chapters, I progressed to another addiction and soon learned all about the drug that took me down this path and inspired me to write this book: my new best friend, cocaine—the "Devil's Candy."

I was around plenty of drugs at fraternity parties all the time in college, but never had any intention of actually using them. At thirty-one, I had only tried marijuana five or six times and had never fallen into smoking or drinking. I was a nerdy prude until the day came when I met cocaine face to face. Cocaine took me down hard and fast.

My very dear college friends Joanie and Paula took me out on my birthday to cheer me up, and soon we had a routine that progressed to dancing at Midnight Rodeo on Thursday and Saturday nights. I was having fun being single again and met Robbie, my bridge to the other side. He asked me to teach him to dance, and he in return would buy my drinks. Seven months later we were still dancing. He was cute and funny, and he thought I was pretty and smart and fun to be around. Men always know just what to say to "win" us over when we are vulnerable, don't they? It was great to have someone so interested in me again.

I was left feeling very down about myself, and I was enjoying the attention and fuss Robbie made over me. He started spending a lot of time around me and the girls. I surprised him for his birthday with tickets to a Dallas Cowboy's football game my brother Damon gave me, and on our twelve-hour drive to Dallas, he pulled powdered cocaine out, rolled up a dollar bill and snorted it and told me to try some. At first I said no, but I was in such a fragile and vulnerable state I decided, what the heck. Regrettably, I tried it and bingo . . . I was instantly taken to a place where adultery, alcoholism, peer pressure, verbal abuse, perfectionism, image, responsibility, hardship, and pain didn't even exist. I'd never been so serene, comfortable, and content, and I loved it. Wow, why hadn't I known about this before? I momentarily forgot (avoided) all my problems, but sadly realized I ignored the simple laws of physics that *WHAT GOES UP MUST COME DOWN*.

CHAPTER FIVE

COCAINE, MY NEW BEST FRIEND

At different stages in life, we will all seek to escape painful moments or tragedy. When I thought I had hit the bottom, I found myself with a new best friend. One in all my years I would never have expected: cocaine. Finally, I had found loyalty and commitment. Have you ever chosen something you knew was wrong, but you felt so low you thought you had nothing to lose? Have you misplaced your trust in somebody only to be betrayed? Do you feel like a failure for choosing so poorly? When there's a deficit, it can drag you in even deeper, making you feel as if you will never be happy or successful again.

Being under the influence of cocaine could never truly be described on paper, nor would I want in any way to glorify its usage. For purposes of understanding my poor decisions in life, I want to describe the pleasure it falsely brought to me. Addiction in all forms will ALWAYS win over husbands, children, parents, jobs, morals, values, and even self-preservation. For me, nothing was more important than my cocaine addiction. It took a life-changing rock bottom experience and a loss of life for me to stop. I've heard about physical, emotional, and spiritual addiction, and I now know that this was insidious, and eventually uncontrollable. I could have controlled the first step and not tried the cocaine, but after I became addicted it was impossible to control.

I believe I was truly possessed during my addiction because no amount of strength, self-will, meetings, rehabs, or medication could free me from the enslavement. Oh, I wanted desperately to stop. Each time I cried for help, put myself in rehab, or made a deal with God, I meant every word. I really wanted to stop, but just couldn't. I was simply going through the motions of life numb and merely existing, no longer living real life or thriving.

I remember studying in college about rats in captivity and how given a choice between food and cocaine, they would choose cocaine every time, even to the point of starvation and death. You can never understand the insanity around this theory until you live it. I understand it all too well now. As my addiction progressed, I became very self-destructive. It was a slow painful death for my loved ones to watch. I quit eating, socializing, and parenting. I'd spend hours behind a locked bedroom door hiding in paranoia or maintaining my high. The actions taken to stay in a false sense of security are things you can never take back. These shady, manipulative, and demeaning acts will haunt us forever. After many years of those things keeping me in a food addiction and self -destruction mode, I finally found a key to stop letting those things define who I am now. I have started embracing those memories as fuel to help others avoid their pitfalls by sharing my story. The old mantra "sharing is caring" has proven rewarding for me because I am using my experiences to help others, and now I see something positive to reflect on instead of dwelling on the negativity of my past.

I started snorting lines (rails) of cocaine on weekends or when my kids were out of the house. Everything was heightened to a new level on cocaine. I felt a sense of pleasure I'd never experienced, and all the problems seemed to be far, far in the distance. Instead of focusing on bills, responsibilities, my ambitions, or my duties, the cocaine provided a false euphoria, and those things were no longer in the forefront of my mind.

Have you ever felt like your mind was so cluttered with stuff it made choosing one thing to accomplish overwhelming?

Finally, my constantly busy mind could relax. My mood was carefree, and sex was better because under the influence of a mind-altering substance, I was deceptively happy and would completely let go and have no inhibitions or insecurities. I became loud, bold, and selfish. The small-town popular beauty queen was a monster inside but still under the disguise of a tiara and sash. Nobody knew- the deception felt devious and I liked "getting away" with fooling everyone that I was a good girl. Sadly, I had no idea what obstacles I was about to face ahead of me. I was charging blindly full blast ahead on a self-destructive path. In a brief moment when the stress and anxiety of life faded away, I was lost to addiction that fast. What I didn't know about addiction is it changes those around you too. When you become a slave to the pipe, rail, bong, or bowl, your inner circle gets sucked into the manipulation, lies, and legal matters as well. Addiction is a jealous creature and does not like to share.

CHAPTER SIX

BECOMING AN ADDICT

I began to think that life was too good to be true and that I'd never have a honest, lasting relationship. The stability I thought I had was fading.

After a few months, Robbie started disappearing two to three days at a time. His personality had changed, and he was becoming verbally abusive and would tell me he loved me one day and couldn't stand me the next. I was allowing *his* mood to determine *my* happiness just like I had let Eric. He would call me crying and ask for help. I had no idea what he needed help from, just that he needed help. I couldn't understand his desperation then, but I now sympathize and pray for every addict under the bondage of any addiction because it is cruel, enslaving, and demanding, and it strips us of all control. Robbie had started "rocking" the powder and making crack, which is a solid form of cocaine you smoke. I was fed up with his disappearing acts and asked what was so wonderful about it, pointing out that he risked losing me, Lauren, and Amber.

When the girls were gone for summer break, Robbie brought crack to my house, and I tried it. Being I'd never been a smoker before, I had a hard time getting the smoke into my lungs. This drug requires a precise technique of firing the pipe and inhaling gently after the heat is removed.

Of course, I am a perfectionist, so kept at it until I had the technique conquered and had then become a full-blown crack addict and wasn't even aware of the enslavement I was soon to be under. When someone says, "You'll be hooked after the first hit," don't take that lightly. It is a true statement of reality. I was naïve to think I wouldn't become addicted. I told myself I wouldn't because I'd never smoked cigarettes and didn't even drink coffee! I was up against a battle I was statistically destined to lose. I didn't realize I was already an addict of men, sex, overeating, and over-achieving. I was fooled to think I couldn't become an addict to cocaine and didn't realize I was a different woman now. I had become a broken, scorned, depressed, and cynical woman looking for comfort from any-thing or anyone. Back in college, I had turned my head away from drugs time after time again, but not now; drugs had me in a chokehold. My vul-nerability provided an open gate for it to take complete control of my life. Why do we think we know it all? How come I was so gullible? I blame my naivety on years of a protected and sheltered life. Looking back I real-ize the hold it had on him and wonder why he would even let me try it.

I went through several rehabs and heard different medical theories about people being predestined or genetically inclined to be addicts. As for me, it was definitely exposure to the drug at the "right" time in my life. I was depressed, vulnerable, mad, hurt, disappointed, scorned, failed at a ten-year marriage, and feeling sorry for myself. Seriously, what person wouldn't welcome a "fix" that took all those things away momentarily? What I failed to realize is when I came down from my oblivious high, I was still all those things, but now I was even more — I was a crack addict too! Me, Mistie. How, when, why??? Oh, God, HELP ME. What goes up must come down, and I was crashing fast and hard.

We started smoking crack at night after the girls went to bed. Then we could no longer wait until they fell asleep, and we started taking turns going into the bathroom while cooking dinner, doing their homework, or during their baths. I was able to maintain my job at the hospital, but finally the staying awake three and four nights in a row was catching up to me. I was nodding off in front of my patients and running home during lunch to get high just to be able to stay awake and get through the rest of the day.

I progressed to running to the parking lot between patients to take a couple of "hits" in my car and lying down on the hospital bathroom floor taking catnaps. My life and career were unraveling, and my parents, friends, and children sensed it. They watched me deteriorating but didn't know what to do. I wanted so badly to cry out for help, but I was convinced I was strong enough to fix this myself. Some may ask, "Where was your God?" Let me assure you, God was there with me always, or I wouldn't be alive today writing my testimony. God was watching me and crying the entire time waiting on me to reach up and grab His hand. Instead, I turned my back on Him and played into Satan's hand. I was brainwashed and fooled into thinking my help came by way of inhaling white smoke through a glass pipe, which only momentarily relieved my pain. Satan doesn't look like the stereotypical horned creature in a red cape to me; instead Satan is a glass pipe filled with dope pouring out white swirly whimsical smoke. I still get nauseated or "triggered" just by seeing white cigarette smoke twirling and twisting in the air when someone blows it out their car window or I walk by and see the cloud of smoke still dancing around. Being a slave to crack is like what I imagine hell to be.

When I have flashbacks of "missions" and Satan deceivingly glorifying those times, I pray for God to show me the flip side of my kids crying themselves to sleep at night because mommy didn't come home again. When I remind myself of the pain, God removes the craving or memory. It is still a battle eleven years out, even after my tragedy, but I keep it real and fight every day to be the best I can.

If you're in this fight against a hopeless situation too, just know that you can win the battle. YOU ARE NOT ALONE!

I pray you can find inner strength to let God (or your higher power) fight your battles too. All you have to do is ask! Decide today to PULL YOURSELF UP. I am sharing my story in hopes you will realize you can beat addiction— it isn't easy or appealing at first, but I beg you not to end up like me with an unthinkable occurrence that can never be taken back. In reality, there is no "extra life," or we can't "one-up" from the dead to keep playing the video game—real-life death is permanent.

The bondage of addiction is the most powerful thing I've ever encountered. The strongest, bravest, and smartest person won't "win" against drugs by thinking they can quit when they want. Don't believe your own LIES! I don't know how many binges started by me saying "I'll just smoke one rock and quit" . . . or "Just one last party." Maybe at first, but eventually the drug owns us. It progresses with jealousy and persistence until our own identity is gone, and we are just walking zombies with hearts full of resentment, anger, embarrassment, and shame. People change, and it's difficult to know you're changing until you do. I transformed into someone I'm not.

As a young mother at twenty-one, I was a Christian and believed in God but didn't know or trust Him. I was afraid to even hang a crucifix over Lauren's baby bed in fear the devil would say, "There goes one, let's go after her." I thought if I stayed "neutral" the devil wouldn't mess with me or her. I now realize how unprotected I was for not having faith God would protect us. The only way out of hell for me was turning everything—I mean everything—over to God. Every worry, burden, pain, guilt, shameful memory, and insecurity had to be addressed. This is not a simple task, and it's easy for us to become doubtful and take it all back on ourselves. But, the releasing is what sets us free. Try it. I know you are thinking, *Yeah, right!*, but I'm telling you, in order to move on with your life, you must let it all go. There is a simple sense of freedom when you actually physically do it. STOP reading and take time for yourself to write it all down. Write down your ambitions and how you let them slip away. Write down your biggest fears and how you failed at ever confronting any of them, write down your deepest intimate secrets nobody knows, write down your anger towards people—then burn or flush the list. The simple physical act of "tossing" this stuff out provides a release that allows you to start rebuilding. It sounds trivial, but seriously, trust me and put this book down and do it. This is your FIRST STEP TO PULLING YOURSELF UP!

Lauren sent me a letter in jail and told me to make a list of all the things that haunt me and flush it. My kid was parenting ME. She is full of wisdom, and I am blessed beyond measure as this was my first step to feeling I *could* rebuild my life and coexist with my shameful memories by releasing the guilt.

Addiction encompassed so much of my life I don't even know where to begin. I was forced by cravings to be a slave to my pipe all day and all night, no matter what. It was so jealous I couldn't even leave it alone long enough to give my child a birthday party, show up on time to pick them up from practice, sit through an entire movie with them, or even make it through a shower without taking a hit. Complete enslavement. What was the attraction in spending all my money on something that made me spend all my time locked behind doors or peeking through windows out of paranoia? Pure craziness. Looking back I can see the power the drugs had over me. It sounds ridiculous. Doesn't it?

Cocaine was my everything, and I had become completely dependent on it to make me numb to anything I didn't want to feel. I became pregnant and decided on an abortion due to the fact I couldn't even take care of myself. I took a hit in the car going into the abortion and took a hit the minute I got back in the car like I didn't even skip a beat, completely emotionless to what I had just done!

My heart was truly broken, and the pain was severe, but I never faced it and kept shoving it deeper and deeper down inside, covering it up with hit after hit. Cocaine magically convinced my mind to ignore what I had just done, but like I said, "What goes up must come down," and when I crashed, I totaled myself. I tried desperately to clean my life up and would be successful one month, even two or three months, but the grief, guilt, pain, shame, blame, and depression only steered me right back into the arms of my numbing partner, cocaine-EVERY time. After all, I could count on cocaine; it was loyal, trustworthy, and always there for me.

Later, I had another abortion, and cocaine got me through that one too. I started justifying my usage of cocaine or started justifying an abortion because of cocaine. Do you see a trend here? The pain MUST be dealt with. All pain that dwells in our gut, heart, and head must be released. A grieving process is healthy and necessary to get through the shame and guilt. I was tormented by replaying those events over and over, and it would eventually cause me to relapse momentarily to ease my pain. The abortions are further addressed in the chapter "The Insanity Begins" because you will not believe what I did or didn't do. This loss of life became an even bigger loss with one bad decision leading me into a deeper dark hole. Piece by piece, hit by hit, I was slowly vanishing away, almost unrecognizable to the ones that knew and loved me.

I was lost, tossed, and out of control. I know after my abortions I always felt anger at my family, myself, God, the doctor, and the man responsible. I felt pressured to have an abortion by my family and betrayed by people demanding I abort to avoid shaming *them* with an illegitimate child. Deep-rooted resentments formed around the pressure from my family. They had my future interest in mind, but still, how do you tell somebody to abort a child?

Other addictions were apparent such as using food as comfort, sexual addiction, constantly having to get others' approval, and being a people pleaser. I am thankful I was able to escape bulimia at age thirty-one because I was so desperate to look perfect I tried to induce vomiting one night. I strained so hard I burst blood vessels in my eyes and looked evil and scary for four days. Panicked, I called the emergency room and was told it would clear up in a few days, but I was fortunate I was unable to start the very deadly cycle of binging and purging. Although I knew they were right, I was angry because I felt I couldn't even be a bulimic right. Yet another failure!

Many addictions consume us, but I feel all of them are just filling a void space in our heart and soul. I felt deficient in love for the Lord, which is truly where inner peace is rooted. The Word feeds hunger, comforts our minds, and teaches us to give our burdens and worries over to God if we will just SURRENDER to Him. I knew for me, God was my only chance up against the devil. You cannot fight an enemy you can't see on your own.

What will save you? Do you truly turn it over to God or your higher power? Find something to believe in and jump in feet first to do the work needed to save yourself, because I promise you, addiction only ends two ways: you die, or someone else will.

CHAPTER SEVEN

THIN LINE BETWEEN LOVE AND HATE

Early in my addiction I met Jerry, a wanna-be gangster from New Jersey. I'd never been with a "tough" guy and really liked his status as a dealer in the drug world. I was drawn to him because he truly seemed to care that I was stuck smoking crack because he knew I had so much going for me. He had been addicted ten years of his life already and tried to warn me of the upcoming destruction. Well, if you can't beat them, join them. He taught me that an addict will pull a clean (drug-free) person down before they will ever lift an addict up. He charmed me like I'd never been charmed. He seemed to geniunely care about me.

I remember the exact moment I fell in love with him. We had been staying in a hotel while my girls were on Easter vacation with Eric, and I was either going in late to work or not going at all due to smoking crack 24/7. I started crying because I saw my life was really spiraling out of control, and he called me over to the window seat in our suite and held me in his arms, rocking me, and he said the Serenity Prayer: "God grant me the serenity to accept the things I cannot change, the courage to change the things I can, and the wisdom to know the difference." I had never heard it before, and as I gazed into his beautiful mesmerizing blue eyes as he wiped my tears, my heart melted. Did he ever really love me or was I just a resource of money for him?

Did I really love him or did I love the attention he gave me? My self-esteem was so low from my marriage ending and my allowing Robbie to make me feel "bad" about myself and always feeling inadequate. Was I just clinging to a man who really understood what I was going through? I believe in my heart he loved me the best he knew how. He and I had so much love and hate between us and really affected each other's lives treacherously. Where do I even begin? Our relationship was extremely TOXIC to each other and family around us. We were volatile, ready to explode with every tic of the bomb (or hit off the pipe).

I wanted to run away from the drug and tried to cure my addiction by doing what counselors call the "geographical" move. I flew to Austin, Texas, for an interview and was offered a nuclear medicine job. I was given twenty-one days to relocate and report to work. The night I arrived back in Albuquerque, Jerry called and asked for a ride. That is the night he started manipulating me, I just wasn't privy to it yet.

After he and I spent several days getting high together, we became inseparable. I decided because he also wanted off the drugs that I would just take him to Austin with me and my girls. Was I crazy? I'd only been with him about five weeks and didn't even really know him. He was a known drug dealer; why would I bring him to Austin and even let him around my kids? I was so far into the addiction that the drug was playing games with my mind and I justified every bad move and choice we made. Drugs affect our logic and our addiction makes decisions for us. Looking back, it makes me angry I ever allowed anything to control me, other than me.

I called Eric and informed him we were moving to Austin, and he actually came to Albuquerque to help me pack up the house. He was finally being supportive and trying to help after realizing what his walking out on us had done. One night while Eric was there, I knocked over a glass of water on the end table and never even wiped it up. Eric later told me he knew right then something was wrong. I had always been so neat, almost to the point of being obsessed with it so he knew I wasn't myself when I didn't clean the water on the table. Jerry and I left while Eric was there with the girls and started smoking crack and didn't even go home that night. The next morning my mom and Bill were at my house worried about where I had been, and when Jerry and I pulled into the driveway, Bill took one look at Jerry and tried running him off with a baseball bat. I was high and thought, *How dare he—that was my house!* They knew he wasn't the type of guy that held a job, went to church, and volunteered around town. Jerry convinced me to leave with him, and I wanted to stay high, so I did. Eric took our girls and left and went back to Texas with them until I could get moved. He was mad I ran off with this druggie and left him there, so he decided not to help me. I don't blame him. I left him at my house and wasn't even packing while he took time off work to help me. By now, everyone knew that something was definitely wrong and that I was in big trouble. They all tried reaching out to me, but I was under two influences—crack cocaine and Jerry.

He had a way of twisting things and convinced me my family was overly judgmental and treated him unfairly. The Mistie before drugs would have listened to my loved ones, but now I was defensive and protecting my habit by staying with Jerry. I had no idea he would soon be giving me bruises up and down my body, breaking my nose, and holding me hostage. How could I be so blind and actually allow all of this to happen to me? The love quickly turned into pure hatred. Are you reading this thinking to yourself, *Oh, I'd never let things get that bad?* Don't fool yourself. Bad becomes worse, and then before you know it, you are stuck at the bottom of a pit searching for a way out. Again I say to you, "Look up, ask for help because there is a way out." You must start focusing on positive instead of negative and not wait until something unbearable happens to make you realize the path of destruction you are on.

Please heed my warning, take *action* now. Do everything you can to fight your addiction.

CHAPTER EIGHT

THE INSANITY BEGINS

I was trying to get the hell out of town and run from this bondage, and thankfully my mom allowed me to put the rental of a Ryder moving van on her American Express. The truck sat in my driveway four days before we even started packing because we couldn't stop smoking dope long enough. We eventually started driving the moving truck around, getting high in it. Finally, we started packing, and he and I packed my entire three-bedroom, two-car garage home, complete with washer, dryer, full house of furniture, swing set, trampoline, tons of boxes of clothes, papers, and toys. Fueled by our high, we stayed awake for hours packing. He loaded every bit of it by himself with a dolly.

We started moving the big stuff around 2 a.m., unconcerned about my neighbors possibly being disturbed by the noise the dolly made going up and down the ramp. I would never have been so inconsiderate if it wasn't for me being high. We drove away from the quaint little cul-de-sac where I had raised my girls for seven years, never to return. I lost a piece of me the day Eric and Bimbo #1 drove out of there, and now another piece was chiseled away with our leaving. Addiction always seems to end up with leaving or being left.

We spent all our gas money for the trip on crack before we left and didn't even care how we would get there because the only thing important was where our next "hit" was coming from to sustain our high. I remembered that while moving my dresser, I found a Texaco card Damon had given me when I was in college to use for emergencies. You can imagine what happened next with that Texaco card! We pulled out of Albuquerque and made a stop across the valley on the west side to one of our dealer's houses to get enough dope to keep us awake on our fourteen-hour drive.

We were pulling my Jeep Grand Cherokee I had bought myself a year ago as a graduation present that Bill had co-signed for. When my demand was outweighing my supply and I didn't pay my car note, my brother Kenny put a couple of my Jeep payments on his credit card to keep it from being repossessed. My family was always supportive and there to rescue me when I needed them. I wish now they would have all let me fall flat on my face and maybe I would have snapped back then instead of taking ten years of devastation and a tragic accident to get me to wake the hell up. They loved me and thought they were "saving" me. They continued with more enabling because I was a master manipulator and convinced them of my lies. What would you sacrifice for love? I've seen it. I've seen my family members sacrifice their money, peace, and time.

Jerry placed boxes of dishes and the back seat from the Jeep onto the curb while arranging for our gerbil to ride safely with air. We took off and left them on the curb without even realizing it. After we got across town, Jerry noticed my Jeep was no longer attached behind us to the moving truck. We panicked and started backtracking. My biggest fear was that it fell off and caused a wreck and may have even killed someone. We tracked all the way back to the cul-de-sac our dealer lived in and there sat the Jeep. It wasn't secured properly and had rolled off the dolly and ended up against the curb without hitting anything. How lucky was that? Jerry hooked the Jeep back up, and we still forgot the seat and the boxes on the curb—insane. I can't believe how oblivious I walked around, high without regard to my surroundings. I said "lucky," but I do realize now that God was protecting us.

We got two hours away and were already getting low on dope, so we became anxious and panicked. The worst thing an addict can do is watch their supply dwindle without means for re-upping it. We were so high and irrational that we turned around and drove all the way back to Albuquerque. Panic strikes when the dope is gone and we go in "mission" mode to re-up. We had no cash, so we sold Jerry's pager full of his clientele to another dealer and also pawned my wedding ring set from Eric and got $150.00. We bought dope with every penny and left again. This time when we ran out, we were able to get rid of all the paraphernalia and keep driving. We were using Damon's Texaco card for fuel and food. I must give Jerry the credit here because he refused to find more dope and found strength to throw everything away and keep driving.

Craving another hit so badly and fighting the fatigue as we were coming down, we pulled over at a roadside park and slept in the cab of the truck. We slept for hours. When we awoke we felt proud we had been able to leave crack behind and felt victorious over our addiction. Finally, we made it to Austin but had no money for a place to sleep. We managed to get his parents to buy us a room one night and my mom to buy us a room another night on their credit cards over the phone. We used room service to eat so it could all be charged to their cards and of course never repaid any of it. I hadn't talked to my new employer on the phone for over a week. They kept calling asking when I would arrive, and I had given them the runaround about not being able to sell my house and needing more time. The last week, I completely avoided all of their calls due to my paranoia and not having an excuse why I hadn't reported. I would wait until after hours and call back and leave a voicemail so I wouldn't have to talk to anyone. Again, my mind was convinced by the drug this was okay and I would still have the job waiting on me.

I had gotten some sleep, eaten, hydrated and was coming back to life, so I reported to my job; that's what I moved there for. I had taken way beyond the twenty-one days to report, and they were no longer offering me the position, which meant I also wasn't receiving the $3,000.00 sign-on bonus promised upon my arrival. Now we were left living out of a Ryder truck still on my mom's credit card with no job, no house, and no money. I was told about another large hospital in Austin that was looking for someone in nuclear medicine. I went and interviewed and not only got the job, but because I also held a BS degree, I was hired as the supervisor to run the department. Remember, once all cleaned up I never looked like a drug addict, and my book was always judged by my cover. I earned a great salary, and they offered a $5,000.00 sign-on bonus. My first pay check was to include the first $2,500.00 and the rest was to be dispersed over the next year. Consequently, I landed on my feet as I always did and didn't suffer any real consequences at the time. Meanwhile, our families were out money from helping us get there, and my kids were still with Eric. How could I have let that happen? It is monstrous to consider. The only answer is that a drug you never think can change you, did. I tried it once, and then my life was forever changed.

We found a beautiful brick home in an upper middle-class neighborhood, and my dad agreed to wire us the deposit money with my promise of repaying with my sign-on bonus. Of course, we never did. We unpacked the van and started setting up our beautiful home. Jerry worked diligently, trimming our yard, edging and grooming the lawn, and arranging my big canopy swing by the front porch. We appeared a normal household and had a few wonderful months pretending we were. We could have been happy there playing family complete with a swimming pool and dog. "Could have, would have, should have," famous words.

The girls came back from Eric's and we set their rooms up and enrolled them in school. Lauren was in sixth grade at a brand new middle school that was just built, and Amber was in third grade. Things were really good for a few months. Jerry started his own lawn service named "From the Ground Up" and got his dad to co-sign a rather large commercial mower tractor. I remember taking the girls swimming at Travis Lake and making a comment about getting high. Jerry picked me up and threw me in the water and said, "Are you crazy?" That woke me up, and I realized how stupid it even sounded. We are supposed to be "geographically cured."

I started noticing how possessive and jealous Jerry was. He was telling me how to dress and making accusations about me and the two men I supervised at the hospital. I hadn't been with him sober functioning in the world before. The only Jerry I knew was the one in the hotel room with me getting high, having sex, and floating around town in a parallel world. We stayed mostly isolated and never really interacted with other people, so I had never seen this antisocial side of him. I began to think that he was not who I wanted him to be. Was he like that all along? Or, was it the drugs that covered up his paranoia?

Damn, he is really whacky! The things he dreamt up. He was so insanely jealous that when I opened the kitchen mini blinds in the morning, he thought I was signaling the neighbor to come screw me or something. I mean, his thought process was really out there. If he felt I was a whore just screwing everyone, why was he with me? He didn't even allow me and my girls to go to Wal-Mart alone because he didn't trust me. He started looking at my beeper and going through my purse. I'd never been around this type of obsessive jealousy before. It all stemmed from his own guilt, and he assumed others were like him. Later, he actually picked up a woman in the Wal-Mart parking lot, paid her $10.00 to screw, and ended up with a STD because of it. No wonder he didn't want me to go alone. I didn't know that world and was baffled and resentful of his accusations. I was completely monitored and controlled by him by this time and didn't really see the situation as it was.

It all came to a head one night when I was lying on the floor in our bedroom, and out of the blue he threw the very large and thick Austin, Texas, yellow pages phone book straight down on my face. What was this? I had never been around physical abuse before but was pretty sure it was happening to me. I threw him out and said for him to go back to New Jersey. I wasn't going to allow a man to mistreat me like that. I took him to the bus station and dropped him off. Of course, his family in New Jersey didn't really want him either because he had burned all his bridges with them. Later that evening he returned pleading his case with dramatic apologies, concern, and crack cocaine. I was shocked, in pain, and out of my element and let him back in and started getting high all over again. The drug was his control over me; he knew it and used it very strategically to pull me back under his control. This never ends well, and I was destined to self-destruct. I spent a $1,800.00 paycheck in five days, and the violence was creeping back slowly. It started with a simple push, and then he'd grab my arm so tight he'd leave finger mark bruises on me. He would belittle me by calling me names and saying I was a whore and anything else he could say to bring me down. The vicious domestic violence cycle was part of my life now, and I didn't even realize it. Days of abuse followed by remorse, love, apologies, and promises kept me on an emotional roller coaster. Again, I was depending on someone else's mood to determine MY happiness. When he would become angry, I saw evil in his eyes and genuinely feared him. How could those beautiful blue eyes turn to become empty and threatening?

I was loyal to him and far from a whore, yet he spit in my face once because someone called our house as a wrong number, and he assumed it must have been for me! He even smelled my underwear when I'd come home. This type of obsessive suspicion was because HE was guilty. My first black eye came, and I told the girls a box fell off the shelf and hit me, but Lauren was too smart for that. At eleven she said "Mama, he's no good, and he will probably hurt you real bad one day." Kids are so perceptive and really can measure a person up from the first encounter. I couldn't see it because he was manipulating me with cocaine and keeping me high all the time. I wanted out. I needed out, but I was scared to leave.

Things were progressively worse and we started writing checks from an old closed account Eric and I had a couple of years prior. We wrote $9,681.00 worth to be exact. Jerry forged about $4,500.00 with Eric's name, and I was racking up bounced "unworthy" checks all over Texas. A couple of years later I turned myself in to clear my conscious and do the right thing, so I was allowed to pay restitution in lieu of jail time. As usual, Jerry never answered to any of it, and I got the charge. If he were a real man, he would step up to the plate and take accountability instead of sending me to the butcher's block. Of course, a real man wouldn't be giving me black eyes either. I was so stupid to always protect him. Why don't we choose to learn from our mistakes? I went back to him repeatedly even knowing how TOXIC he was to me and my kids.

As the addiction consumed more and more of my time, my job became endangered, and I quit after being asked to take a drug test. They escorted me immediately from the hospital. I worked twelve years in college for this? What a waste of knowledge and earning potential. I was becoming a woman full of anger, hostility, rage, and resentment and completely dove head first into numbing my pain. Eventually, we were leaving the girls at home for longer periods of time after school so we could drive around and smoke crack. We even "forgot" to drop off lunch money at Lauren's school a few times leaving her to ask, borrow, beg, or just go without lunch. This memory haunts me and breaks my heart because we had plenty of food at home, but I was in too big a hurry to make her a lunch because we needed to score dope. Amber's lunches were prepaid by the month, thank God. The mommy they had known to be protective, loving, and responsible had left them alone and completely checked out, leaving them to fend for themselves during this period! How did I check out so easily? When I passed by a mirror I no longer saw myself. I wasn't there. Mistie no longer existed. This person in my shell was selfish, uncaring, and out of control. I WAS SCARED OF HER!

Realizing things were only getting worse and the violence was more frequent, I found the courage to put myself in a rehab for the first time. Eric had separated from PSYCHO Bimbo #1 after their son was born and agreed to take the girls so I could put myself in a twenty-eight-day rehab. I called my dad to come get me. He didn't know exactly what was going on but knew something definitely was. He and Barbara arrived and saw my house was upside down, and the hot water was disconnected. He couldn't believe this was his daughter's house (Ms. Perfectionist). I confessed to them for the first time I was using cocaine and needed help. They were devastated and, of course, blamed Jerry. What man would allow all of this to happen? Dad was even more upset at the bruises he noticed on my arms. He and Jerry had a physical confrontation, and I instantly realized what we were all up against.

We agreed Dad and Barbara would get a hotel room, and we would go to dinner and discuss our plans to pack up the house and get me into rehab. I gave my Dad my paycheck of about $1,600.00 and asked him for only $100.00. I begged him to let Jerry and me rent our own room and spend one last night together. He agreed, and we were all to meet at our house at 6 a.m. to start packing. Of course, Jerry and I started hitting the dope and ran off for ten days never returning to that house or calling anyone to let them know we were alive. At this time we had rented a vehicle on my mom's American Express because we drove my Jeep into the ground and dropped the transmission, leaving my co-signer Papa Bill to fininsh paying the debt.

We left the entire house for my Dad and Barbara to pack up and put in storage. Thank God they didn't just say to hell with it and get rid of my stuff. They should have. Both of my parents packed and moved me about six times while I was in jail or missing in action. I always knew they would "rescue" me and depended on it, so I felt running away would never have any real or severe consequences. My family didn't realize they were only enabling me by always picking up my pieces to protect me, my credit, my job, my reputation, and my record. As addicts, we *need* to fall on our face to wake us up. If you are an enabler of somebody wanting help, I suggest letting them fall. Make them feel the degree to which they screwed up, and don't bail them out of jail or any other financial situation. You may think you are helping protect their "future," but in reality, if you keep helping them get away with things, they might not have a "future" to protect!

After ten days, we tried going to my dad's in Southeast Texas but always kept going back to Austin for more dope. I finally called my sister and said, "It's me; am I welcome to go to Dad's?" I was too scared to call him and had no clue what had even happened to my house. During those ten days of missing in action, my mom had spent hours on her hands and knees grieving, scared I was dead somewhere. Both my brothers came to Austin and looked at pawn shops and even staked out our house for a few days looking for me. My dad bought his first cell phone and slept in his car in front of the house, hoping we'd return. They didn't know if I was dead or alive. Honestly, I might as well be dead because I was high 24/7 oblivious to the insanity and the pain I had caused my family.

My sister called my dad, and he said of course for us to come to his house. He was desperate to get me under his protection. Their daughter had turned into someone they didn't even recognize, but they wanted to help me. They loved me. They played along by letting Jerry come just to get me home safely.

We pulled into my dad's early in the morning, and all I wanted to do was have him take me to Lauren and Amber's bus stop so I could see them. I missed them terribly, and after coming down realized what I had done. My dad said, "Baby it is Saturday." I honestly thought it was Wednesday—that is how lost I truly was. Insanity? I was four days off. I had come down enough to realize I was in severe trouble and needed help. I wanted help. I found a twenty-eight-day live-in rehab in Beaumont, and my dad took me there. Jerry refused rehab, so my dad spent $800.00 putting him on a one-way plane to New Jersey. He actually flew first class because that was the only thing available and my dad was desperate to get him away from me.

I was learning about the drug that stole my identity and because my family was extremely supportive, they were there learning too. I constantly heard them saying, "NOT MISTIE." They always held me high on a pedestal and expected more from me. I resented all the pressure from them. I mean, why NOT Mistie? I guess I showed them! To further complicate the situation, I found out I was pregnant with Jerry's child during my second week of rehab.

One day Eric brought the girls to visit and he sat me down, held my hand, and said "This is all my fault." He wanted to build a house and bring me back home where he thought I belonged. He offered to raise my child with me and wanted his family back. I still loved him, but he broke my heart, and my pride got in the way. When I said no and chose to go back to a drug-dealing abusive felon, Eric turned on me like a snake and barely spoke to me for years after that. I guess his pride got in the way too.

I was pregnant with my son Austin and thought God sent him to "save" me. There was no way I was going to do drugs while pregnant or go through another abortion. (Not then anyway.) Somehow, I convinced myself a baby would cure us, and the drug addiction and physical violence would just vanish. I ran to Jerry in New Jersey after he sent me a Greyhound bus ticket. He traveled first class on an airplane and I rode a bus three days while pregnant with no money for food. Par for the course, I guess.

When I arrived in New Jersey, things went sour between us after he started hitting me again. I couldn't believe it. I was pregnant with HIS only child, and this sick bastard was bruising me up again, and I was *allowing* it. He was arrested on old warrants when the police knocked on our door at the Trump Marina in Atlantic City. Apparently, an ex-girlfriend was jealous and reported our whereabouts, and he was wanted, so they came for him. HATERS! I was left all alone there and managed to make it back to his parents' house in Trenton. I called my dad to bring me home and he said no. He was trying to show me tough love, but I conned him into paying my way back home to his house.

Having time to sober up again, I immediately landed another supervisor of nuclear medicine job and moved into another beautiful home. Because of my career, rebuilding was pretty easy for me every time. I got my girls back home with me, and things went well during my pregnancy. My college friend Joanie came to visit from Albuquerque and help me move into our new home. Although Eric was still angry and barely talking to me, for the girls sake, he helped me and Joanie move my stuff from Austin. My fate could have changed right there, but one decision altered it all. Jerry. He was released from jail and managed to once again charm me (he's good) and con me, and I bought him a plane ticket to Texas where he walked right into a beautiful home, money in the bank, and a woman pregnant with his son who thought she loved him.

After I allowed him back, my family pretty much washed their hands of me, including Eric, again. My mom was there as usual and stayed with me near my due date, putting her hatred for Jerry aside for my benefit. Jerry hit me a few times throughout the rest of the pregnancy, but I felt stuck and too beaten down to pull out of it. I convinced myself that Jerry could love me and the baby enough to stop the abuse. Of course, the abuse continued, and he always convinced me it was *my* fault.

For a few months things were good, but I was having trouble with Eric, and we fought over visitations with the girls, child support he wasn't paying, and health insurance costs. Jerry was working with my friends Becky and Jerry, going to church, and we were honestly trying to make it. Then, one rainy day when he was let off work early and I couldn't pick him up on time because I got held up at the hospital, he snapped. Jerry was not to be inconvenienced. He assumed, in his sick, obsessive, and guilty mind that I was whoring around and that's why I was late getting him. Most of his rages stemmed from extreme jealousy, and he didn't perceive things normally. He blamed his behavior on being in prison so many years watching shows like Jerry Springer where women slept with brothers, cousins, fathers, and other family members. He claims the shows warped his view of women. I tried telling him the small groups of women that were on those shows were not representative of the norm. There was no convincing him of anything. Once a psychologist was listening to me describe Jerry's attitude and was actually able to finish my sentences for me. She asked if he had done a lot of time in prison because he fit the characteristics of "Anti-Social Personality Disorder." I got excited and said, "Okay, now we know what he has—what medication will fix him?" Unfortunately, there isn't a pill for it.

As expected with domestic abuse cycles, his violence returned, and I kicked him out. He returned with dope (just like in Austin) and lured me back in. I fell right back into the trap and cycle of him controlling me with the dope. After giving me black eyes, I learned to depend on the high to numb the pain. The swelling and throbbing lasted for days, and he knew he had me right where he wanted me during this time—high! I was breast feeding Austin, and when I relapsed that night I knew I couldn't breast feed him again. My poor son woke up to a bottle of formula, just like that. No gradual weaning, just instant change—this was insanity at its worst, and far from the Mistie everyone knew, loved, and respected.

CHAPTER NINE

YET ANOTHER RESCUE

T hings were quickly going downhill again, and Jerry pawned everything I had of value to get high while I was at work. Why was I allowing so many things to transpire and letting him get away with so much? He wasn't contributing anything financially, he wouldn't get up with Austin in the middle of the night to help me, and he pawned all my belongings. Damon had loaned me a car but came unannounced one night and took it from me because he learned Jerry was driving it. We were left stranded. With the cash from the savings bonds Dad and Barbara had bought the kids every birthday since birth, my 401K Plan (of course Jerry never had a real job), and some money my sister sent, we bought a used car. Jerry never contributed anything to pawn, cash in, or lose. Meanwhile I was being stripped of everything of value, down to my morals. He came empty handed and left me worn down and defeated.

Christmas 2000 approached, and we were writing more hot checks to support our dance with addiction. We bought the kids all kinds of presents, wrapped them, and put them under the tree. Lauren and Amber guessed the two big boxes under the tree were TVs for their rooms. They were right, but a few days later Jerry took them back and got the money, or "clucked" them so we could maintain our high. This happened three different times, and the girls would ask "What happened to our presents?" I don't even remember what we told them, but I'm sure we really confused them and played their emotions. Somehow, we miraculously replaced them, and they did open TVs Christmas morning. Can anyone relate to this insanity? Am I the only one hooked this badly to do this? I had never heard anyone speak of such unfathomable things so assumed I was a MONSTER. If you have done horrible things, please know you are not alone; this is what addiction does. Are you beating yourself up over things you have done under the influence as well? I'm not saying those things are just excused, but if we learn from our life lessons and make a change, the teaching and giving to others takes the focus off the wrong we did.

I knew things were out of control and we were in grave danger after Jerry literally held me and Austin hostage for three days. He went into a rage, ripping the phones out of the walls and removing parts so the car wouldn't run. He smoked all the dope and did not allow me to have any. The cravings were almost unbearable. He was so cruel, and I had PURE HATRED for him now. I knew my fate if we didn't get out. I managed to call daddy again to my rescue while the girls were at their dad's. I had heard when you leave an abuser to be careful not to alert them of your plans to leave. I casually washed our clothes and gathered baby bottles, food, and essential things. When Jerry went into a rage he was dangerous, and I literally feared for our lives. He was like Jekyll and Hyde. I had to wait a long three nerve-wracking hours for my dad to drive to me late that night. I was sitting in the living room and still had my shoes on, and Jerry questioned why I was dressed at 10:00 at night. He ordered me to go change and take off my shoes. Already paranoid, now he was on to me. After not being allowed any dope for three days, now he WANTED me to get high because he knew that was his control over me. I was ravenous with cravings, and although I knew my dad and the cops would knock on the door any minute, I gave in and got high anyway. Talk about even more insanity.

The knock on the door came pretty quickly after only about four or five hits, so under dad's protection, I was able to stay strong and leave him and the dope. I never realized how scared I was of him until my dad caught me staring out the window of the bedroom of his secluded lake house. He assured me Jerry wouldn't find his house and I was safe. I knew what he was capable of and was scared to death to the point my dad stayed in the room with me, Austin, and a double barrel shotgun.

After three days we returned to my house to pack and once again put my stuff in storage. My mom and Bill had come again to help and take us back to Albuquerque with them. By the time I arrived back at the house, almost everything of value had been taken, including the girls' new radios they had gotten, the microwave, and the car. The girls had moved back in with their dad, but Amber wanted to be with me, so I took her and Austin and left for Albuquerque. I called Eric and asked him to come meet me so we could talk about Amber leaving with me, but he refused to even get on the phone. I felt I had no choice but to take my sweet little Amber, who wanted to be with me. Lauren, already tired of my chaos, chose to stay behind and live with her daddy. I had no idea where Jerry was, nor did I care. I wanted to run from him. (Later, I discovered he was hiding in the attic while we were packing the house up. I guess he wasn't so tough when other people were around.)

Eventually, he stole a truck, drove to New Mexico, and found us in Albuquerque. By the time he arrived, I had been attending church and NA meetings and doing well. Jerry claimed to be sober, back in church, and doing well too so we agreed to meet him at McDonald's so he could see Austin, who was now seven months old.

Eventually I allowed him to brainwash me and believed he loved me and the cocaine was causing him to act like Satan in the flesh. I went to his motel room to surprise him and take him to a NA meeting, and instantly knew he was high when I looked at him. I should have turned around and left and once again gotten rid of him but instead I fell right along with him, just that easily. Like the saying goes, "You will go down with an addict before you can bring them up" We went on a seven or eight-week mission and to spare more insane details, ended up back in the same scenario.

As we were leaving a furniture store where we bought gift cards to swap for dope, he got mad and started beating me and pulling my hair. Satan was back. I demanded he take me to my mom and kids. Before he dumped me in the driveway, he rummaged through my purse, stripped me of all my clothes looking for hidden money, and took anything of value, along with any dignity I had left. He always made sure I returned home with nothing. Somehow, I was always able to muster strength from deep down to call for help when I knew I couldn't stop. I'm glad my parents planted good morals and values in me growing up because I think that is what I clung to when I asked for help. I knew I wanted to stop and wanted to be home with my kids and was able to realize I wasn't in control. At this point I'm not sure what was worse, the crack addiction or domestic abuse. Both had undeniable control over me.

The same afternoon I demanded he take me home, he was surrounded by the ROPE Team (Repeat Offender's Program.) He was in a stolen vehicle and went to prison for five years behind several warrants. He was actually shipped from the jail to prison on Father's Day (his very first one.) How sad. Again, I was protected by angels and spared from that encounter with the police that afternoon. That wasn't chance; God gave me the strength to go home that day and walk away from the next hit. I was left (again) with anger, rage, hostility, resentment, hatred, physical and mental bruises—but alive, free, and home with my family that still loved me. I wish I could give you a formula and say do "this" to walk away from the next hit, beating, or mission. I don't have the magic key. What I can tell you is something very deep inside always gave me enough strength and courage to make that rescue phone call. Find your inner strength and build it and learn to trust and use it—it could very well save your life.

CHAPTER TEN

TO BE LOVED BY A "GOOD" MAN

My vehicle was left on a burglary scene, and Gene (my next husband) was the auto theft detective called for the recovery and investigation. I went to his office for questioning, and I told him my boyfriend had a drug problem and had taken it. He lectured me for being with such a bad man with a long rap sheet and had no idea I was no better. Looks are so deceiving, and again my inner monster was hidden behind my tiara and sash. When we went to the impound yard, we both realized we had met previously. Back in 1999 when I "rented" my Jeep to Jerry for dope, he took off in it for days, and Gene was the detective that found and returned it to me. He came by the hospital where I was working and took my statement a few weeks before I moved to Austin, Texas. We definitely had an attraction then, and excitingly felt it again now. He was handsome and charming, but because he was ten years older than me, I wouldn't go out when he asked. His persistence finally won me over and we began dating. He treated me like a queen and respected me, had intelligent conversations, and actually worked and paid taxes. He came to Austin's first birthday party, and my son and I both fell in love with him. He made me see how mistreated I had been, and his gentleness was so new and welcomed. I wasn't sure if I was in love with Gene or I loved the way he loved me and my kids. I eventually admitted to him I too had a drug problem and several encounters with the law. He believed in me and somehow made me believe in myself for the first time in a long time. I couldn't wait to become his wife because I could say Mrs. Gene "_____" had never done drugs. I was desperately trying to gain my dignity back by creating a new identity not associated with the cocaine gang.

Things were great while pretending to be the happy little family. We got a house, and Lauren came back to live with us. I had all three kids under my roof again, had a job at the hospital, and was doing well. What are you thinking right now? Are you thinking, *Yep, she blew it again*? Have you landed back on your feet from something only to voluntarily dive back full force into HELL? That's a close assessment. The problem is, we never deal with all our junk inside and just hide it or stuff it deep down. If we don't heal the wounds of the past, we bleed all over the ones that didn't even cut us. I allowed Satan to use all my pain against me as a weapon to put me back into the shame and blame game. The story thickens as it gets worse.

Gene and I planned a prepaid, seven-day cruise to the Western Caribbean. Four days before we were to leave, I left work and saw an old dealer in the Wal-Mart line, which led to a relapse, just like that, on impulse. No reason, no premeditated thoughts of using—I just did it spontaneously when he handed me his new number and said, "Just in case." It happens like that. Crack cocaine had found me, was jealous, and not about to share me with Gene. No way . . . NOT WITHOUT A FIGHT.

I was now officially on a mission and when smoking 24/7, it's almost impossible to just put the pipe down and walk away because of the physical and mental cravings. However, on my third night out I managed to at least call Gene for help.

Scared for my safety and well-being, he stayed on the phone with me for two hours while I found my way home. I pulled into our driveway at 4:00 a.m. and our plane was to depart Albuquerque at 8:00 a.m. for Miami. He dropped to his knees, grabbed me, and sobbed tears of joy.

I was safe and made it home. I hadn't been in a healthy relationship and felt truly loved by a "good" man before, but was making sure to ruin it. He spent $300.00 and rescheduled the flight for 11:00 a.m., and of course I immediately passed out from exhaustion and fell into a "crack coma." My mom came over and packed all my stuff for the cruise. I had no idea what clothes she sent, but was thankful she did it for me . . . or for Gene. He deserved this vacation, and they respected and loved him. Any normal person would be so excited to leave for a seven-day cruise, but here I was spending hundreds of dollars on dope hours before departure.

I barely stood through airport security and passed out the minute I sat in the airplane seat. Sleep is imperative and definitely a priority after coming off a mission. I slept, snored, and drooled all the way to Miami, leaving my husband alone without conversation or company, and, I'm sure, embarrassed. We later checked into our hotel where Gene had planned a pedicure, manicure, and massage to surprise me (he always spoiled me), but I was physically unable to go downstairs and do them. Instead, I slept through dinner and again left him alone. The next morning we went to board our ship, but a hurricane at sea delayed our docking. The cruise line gave everyone vouchers to go eat, so we chose Planet Hollywood. After sleep, the next priority is food and hydration, so I ate like a pig, further embarrassing him. This wasn't the sophisticated, well-groomed, loving professional woman he married! I was making a fool of myself and him too. He didn't deserve this; he was a good, law-abiding and loving man.

After binges, our family is so happy to see us alive and home that they cling to us and love on us with relief and gratitude we are safe. However, after a few days, their anger starts setting in, and I could feel the tension between us. Somehow, I was always able to win Gene's forgiveness and convince him I was truly sorry. I pulled off our formal night pictures and didn't even look like I had just smoked $1,000.00 of crack just days before. Looks are deceiving, and I always had a mask to hide my dark passenger behind. That damn mask also served as a curse, allowing me to dig a bigger darker hole to fall in. How did I exist in both worlds simultaneously? I was exhausted just from the mental frustration of it all.

My binges became more and more frequent, and I have countless heartbreaking stories of Gene physically pulling me from crack houses, searching night after night for me, leaving him to be alone with my kids, day after day and night after night. He was an officer of the law and put himself on the line to save me. Due to the ultimate respect Gene deserves, I'll refrain from endless stories of deception and heartache. He was a good man and I'd like to now say, "I'm so sorry for all the pain and huge disappointment I ended up being. I know how much you loved me and you need to know I also loved you. My kids love and respect you too; especially your Li'l Guy, Austin. It wasn't lack of love that made me lose you; it was lack of self-love and self-forgiveness and giving into the temptations to numb all my internal pain. I am so very sorry. Please forgive me."

Our marriage ended when I was kicked out of a twenty-eight-day rehab on the twenty-fifth day for using dope with a girl that brought some in with her. I was smart and knew when on a probation violation I could put myself into a resident rehab and wouldn't go to jail. I found ways to manipulate almost every situation and was really good at being bad. The $20.00 rock of crack drove me to lose my husband (or give him away.) Instead of calling him to come get me and admitting my failure and facing the possibility of jail, the cravings were strong, and instead I called my dope dealer. I stayed gone for two weeks allowing blonde haired, blue eyed Michelle (Bimbo #2) to take over my marriage. Bimbo #2 was my rehab roommate, and I trusted her, but she saw what a good man I had and she went after him when I failed to go home. I don't blame Gene; he was lonely and tired of tracking his wife down. It was hard calling home from jail and hearing her answer my phone at my house. She had nerve enough to tell me to quit calling there when it was my phone she was on, my house she was in, and my husband she was sleeping with in my bed. Gene still visited and brought me money. I know he didn't really want to end our marriage, but he just couldn't handle the chaotic, deceptive, and humiliating life anymore. My first felony was from taking his undercover auto theft truck to the grocery store and staying gone two days. How humiliating; it was his partner randomly called in to process me after I turned myself in. I felt shame and guilt for hurting Gene and jeopardizing his career. This was embarrassing, as these cops were the same ones at our backyard BBQs and wedding party.

After running his reputation into the ground and embarrassing him time and time again, I didn't blame him for hooking up with the alcoholic Bimbo #2 who drank a fifth of Crown Royal every day. He left to save himself, but unfortunately hooking up with someone right out of rehab might not have been the best choice! Poor Gene—he deserves so much better. I wonder what he is running from to keep making poor choices as well. What about you? What are you running from? Now is the time to examine your life and attempt to understand it.

CHAPTER ELEVEN

HOW COULD I?

I ended up staying incarcerated fourteen months on a probation violation, the longest I had ever been away from my family. I was devastated and heartbroken for my kids. I knew by then I could survive the time, but could they? Why should they have to go through this? After all, they had already endured enough strife in their life with me popping in and out. It hurts me I can never rewind the clock and take those painful years away from them, but I believe a silver lining emerged in them learning how every single decision they make has consequences, whether good or bad. My kids are against drugs because they witnessed firsthand the destruction they led to. I hope they keep that attitude and mentality toward addiction throughout their lives. But can it be guaranteed? Of course not. That's their choice to make.

Lauren's high school graduation was two weeks before my release date in New Mexico, so I wrote the judge, and he agreed to release me early so I could go to Texas for her graduation. Two days before my release, the grand jury indicted me on something from four years prior. With this new development, the District Attorney (DA) would not let me leave, and I missed her graduation. I'm sure Lauren was used to coping with all the letdowns in her life, but IT KILLED ME. I swore to make Amber's graduation three years later, but that didn't happen either. When her graduation came about I was once again incarcerated, and sweet, unselfish Amber said, "Mom, it's probably better anyway because it would hurt Lauren's feeling because you weren't at hers." What awesome kids I was blessed with. They displayed UNCONDITIONAL LOVE for me throughout their personal pain, disappointments, and embarrassment. Proudly, after all we went through together, here they are, right alongside me in support of my speaking out with this book.

Let's rewind to the fourteen months I was incarcerated in Albuquerque. Jerry started writing me from prison apologizing for everything and told me how he found God. His letters were all scripture based and full of prayers, so I believed him. I couldn't believe this was the same man. God truly recreated and constructed a man from the scum bag, crackhead, woman beater. After writing him over a year, I was convinced he was a changed man with genuine regrets and apologies. He became a strong emotional pillar for me and always said all the right things with a new-found gentleness, compassion, and love.

He started sending money so I could buy things from the commissary and was very persistent to win me back. He claimed to still love me, and although I had married Gene, he wanted his family back. Bill took time out of his life to make sure Austin went to visit Jerry at the minimum security prison. I was against it at first, but in time realized he was his dad and wanted to be in his life. Bill wanted Austin to know his dad and believed he had turned his life around. What hurts me is they took him to an actual prison to see Jerry, but wouldn't ever let him visit me in a minimum secure prison using an old junior high school as housing and only one perimeter fence. The prison I went to didn't have ANY bars; we literally lived inside the school grounds. I think out of everything, the fact I didn't physically see or touch my kids for two years was the hardest for me, and them! However, I realize I CHOSE THE LIFESTYLE to put myself at the mercy of someone else to see my kids.

Are you willing to do the WORK and find strength to PULL YOURSELF UP before someone else dictates you seeing your kids? This is not a decision anyone else should make for you if you're the parent. Parents lead their children. I had lost my ability to lead.

After all of our writing and sorting through emotions we decided to give our relationship another chance and raise our son together. Although my parents wanted us to wait at least a year before getting together, we did anyway. Are you shocked? Don't judge unless you have walked down a similar path because this is REAL LIFE, and life is hard. I really thought I had fallen in love with this "new" man. We prayed together, cried together, and were making an honest living and building our own family with new furniture, vehicles, habits, and jobs from the ground up. It felt good to actually be beating the odds, so we decided to get married. My dad's preacher friend agreed to wed us at his home. I was afraid to tell my family in fear of their disappointment and disapproval, but I called anyway. I thought my dad was out of town when I only got his voicemail but his friend had called them, and they surprised us and showed up to be our witnesses. Big crocodile tears rolled down my face as I realized my dad had learned forgiveness after starting his own relationship with the Lord. The day my dad stood with me in acceptance of Jerry at my wedding was a proud moment, and I love and respect him and Barbara for being there for me although they anticipated the worse. They were SHOWING me how to forgive and trust the Lord.

Sometimes we miss that message.

Is there someone close to you that tries to SHOW you the way? Does someone walk the path you want? If so, cling to them. I know our first reaction is to run from them because we feel we can't live up to what they ask of us, but instead of running away, try running into their arms and begging them to help you. Our pride gets in the way, or sometimes our shame, but we must cling to those walking straight.

With my job at a local hospital and him working on the pipeline (first real tax-paying job), we rented a cute house and moved to a small Louisiana town. Things were going well, and I broke the news to my daughters on our next visit, and they were leery but also willing to give this "new man" a chance. For a few months we were very happy together. We had a nice Thanksgiving with all three kids and Lauren's boyfriend, Henry (now husband) and set up a beautiful Christmas tree. It was a very memorable day for all of us, as one of the few "normal" moments with Jerry.

But things changed.

Remember everything that goes up must come down? Well, his old behaviors slowly started emerging, and I was allowing him to make me feel ugly, dumb, and worthless or any other characteristic he accused me of being. I knew deep down we were in trouble. It started again when I had worked late at the hospital on call and was only able to fix leftovers for dinner. I had a big turkey leg as the entrée with veggies, salad, and so on. Jerry threw the plate of food and said, "What's this shit?" He did it in front of Austin. I knew HE, the evil Jerry, was back!

He took a trip to New Mexico to report to his parole officer and was pulled over near El Paso, Texas for making an illegal lane change. After running his name, an old warrant appeared, and they arrested him. Although he was faced with adversity, he said he felt so proud that the dope dogs only found his Bible on the front seat. He felt like a survivor! FAKE is what he was. Just because he was off dope and reading the Bible, didn't mean he was living right. His heart and actions had not changed.

I was being told he was facing ten to twenty years and completely lost it. I allowed Satan's temptation to win and ended up smoking crack after going twenty months without it. It only took one little trigger, and cocaine moved right in since Jerry was gone to jail. I picked right back up where I had left off over a year ago, like it was yesterday. I was in trouble, and my family knew it because by now they were privy to all the signs of avoiding phone calls, needing them to watch Austin all the time, lying, and so on.

My dad and Barbara came to stay with me and even drove to El Paso to get Jerry's truck from the impound yard. After getting Jerry a lawyer, he walked out with twenty-two days' credit time served. The day my Dad drove to Austin to pick him up I went to smoke crack after work and left Barbara at my house with Jerry's truck, and she had to pick Austin up from daycare after school. Again, it was always easy for me to run off because I knew others were there to take care of my kids.

I was unable or too scared to go home, and Jerry arrived and immediately came looking for me. He found me, and although I thought he would kill me, he was very supportive, loving, and understanding of why I had relapsed. He tried to help me stop using by staying home three days with me and driving me to and from work and not letting me out of his sight. During these three days I admitted to him I came close to cheating on him during my "mission." He flipped, but remember, he always thought I was a no-good whore anyway. Although he was angry, he surprised me by not getting violent, and we got through it all and decided to stay together. He was nurturing and loving. I believe he was truly trying to change and be the man he envisioned.

After being on recent crack binges, my body craved it, and I had several relapses. I was mad because Jerry was the worst crack head I'd ever been around, yet he was able to say no to it, but I couldn't. I learned in rehab to change my environment and friends because they will drag a sober person down before they could ever be brought into sobriety. I proved this true because soon I had Jerry so frustrated from hunting me down and fighting me, he joined me. We went down together even faster and further than before. Austin was staying with my dad for a week, and we managed to ruin everything we had worked so hard to accomplish. His violence and extreme jealousy returned, and I sported a black eye at work feeling humiliated in front of doctors and peers. Things progressively got worse, and I was full of rage, anger, bitterness, and hatred from his abuse and my own shame. I did some really awful things during this dark time that have HAUNTED ME for years. I admit I did things even I myself can't believe, things I remember saying I'd never do. I was completely enslaved by addiction, and the blame and shame were doing a major number on me mentally. I asked people to forgive me, yet I would relapse and do the same horrible things to my loved ones. I was entangled like spaghetti wrapped intricately in this addiction and couldn't dig my way out. Forgiveness is hard enough on its own, but self-forgiveness is a beast to deal with, and the lack of it kept me wanting to chase my high to stop feeling the pain.

We wanted desperately to stop so we did the famous geographical move again, thinking we could hide from cocaine and find a new town, a safe haven. Jerry landed a pipeline job in Texas, so we set up our RV and I decided to home school Austin. We once again sampled three months of living a normal family life. For me *normal* meant without cocaine, but I was still left constantly dealing with Jerry's extreme jealousy, paranoia, and accusations. With the summer break, I returned to nuclear medicine work at a local hospital. Things were actually looking up, and we were hidden safely away from cocaine in this small RV community spread alongside a beautiful lake.

Unfortunately, I broke my ankle, and the pain was excruciating, so I needed pain pills for sedation. I've never been a pill pusher or abused pain meds, and the Percocet I was given knocked me smooth out. I needed help with Austin, so my mom drove to get us so we could stay with her until I could recover. After a week or so, I had a bad feeling about leaving after Jerrys' personality started showing some familiar signs of relapse. His employer called me, wondering where he was when he stopped answering their calls. BINGO! I knew right then. He had relapsed. I called and asked the manager at the RV park to knock on the door and he said Jerry had been going in and out of the park all night. This was my confirmation he had relapsed, but he tried to convince me he was sick in bed with fever. I knew something was wrong, and honestly hoped he was with another woman so I could drive there and catch him and then have reason (like I needed a different reason) to leave him without internalizing guilt of breaking up our family. If he was with another woman, I could blame him. How many times have you justified someone else's bad behavior for them? Was it out of fear, low self-esteem or just not ready to face the facts? Any sane person would have left over a multitude of other reasons, right? For me, I needed it to be another woman that I physically saw him with, just like with Eric before. When I had a suspicion my partner was cheating, I would convince myself I was paranoid or pretend it wasn't real, but when I physically caught Eric and Bimbo #1 together, that was finally ENOUGH for me to leave him. With Jerry I had justified the beatings, the lying, and the extreme jealousy and stayed with him but knew deep down I needed to leave. I really hoped he was cheating so I could once again have STRENGTH and COURAGE to leave him.

My mom was tired of our games and refused to take me back so I could "catch" him in the act of . . . whatever. I called Lauren to come get me and take me to the RV and told her she couldn't go in because he was contagious with strep throat. She dropped me off and left. Upon opening the door, I instantly knew he was getting high again. I hadn't danced with cocaine for five months, and felt mighty strong against any temptations. Of course, he wanted me to get high with him because he didn't want to stop, but I said no. I asked about another woman being there in my absence, and he confessed to being with prostitutes and smoking $1,000.00 of dope the last week. NOW Satan won. Jerry and Satan knew what would *instantly* reunite me with my best friend. And then boom, with the first hit, the throbbing pain in my ankle vanished, and I became numb to my breaking heart over his cheating.

He made sure to keep me high as to avoid the issue he was sleeping with prostitutes, and I wanted to stay high to avoid him altogether and my once-again failed relationship. The cocaine worked much better than Percocet, and I was walking around on my broken ankle because I felt nothing! I became mentally absent, throwing in the towel to the devil's candy. In just a couple of weeks we went through $5,000.00 and started writing hot checks to support (protect) our high we were now enslaved to 24/7 again. Days turned to a couple of weeks, and I hadn't gone back to get Austin so my mom enrolled him in Catholic school for first grade. I wanted to go to my mom but Jerry always kept me from leaving by threatening me, hiding the keys, or never letting me out of his sight. Mostly, he just made sure to keep me high. I packed a bag and tried to sneak out of the RV while he was sleeping, but he caught me. He was under the bondage of his addiction, and neither of us were strong enough to break away. We both *wanted* to stop; we CRIED, PRAYED, BEGGED, AND EVEN BARTERED WITH GOD to free us of this addiction. We decided to pack the car and just drive and take refuge in hiding at my mom's, hoping we could somehow outsmart cocaine. Sadly, about two miles from her house, the devil found us again, and we turned the car around to get high. We were so close.

Are you judging me right now? What are you thinking? Unless you've lived in panic, paranoia, and the physical angst of needing a hit every five minutes to numb the situation you've just caused, you CAN'T understand it. We just couldn't stop. Satan had a grip on us and wasn't about to let go. Have you ever felt so out of control before? Have you struggled with food, gambling, sex, or porn addiction? Why are we so powerless? I look back and think I must have been possessed to have done those things and continually put myself in dangerous situations. To begin climbing up from your powerlessness, you must find STRENGTH deep down inside from a place you never knew existed and cling to anything that drives you and use it to pull yourself up. Just start slow with one small thing like saying, "I will answer the phone so they know I'm still alive," or, "I will eat something today to nourish myself." After finding something to fuel your desire, cling to it, and eventually you can pull up from your situation, one small thing at a time.

As predicted, our mission was a long one and I just wanted to go home to my kids. I had become tired of the dope scene, full of shame and finally worn down from the abuse. I kept begging Jerry to take me to my mom's house. He wouldn't, so I said, "just let me out of the car!" He squirted cheese whiz all over me, even in my hair, and poured Dr. Pepper on me too, and then he gave me another black eye and said "Get out now. Nobody will pick you up, whore!" I got out, ran behind a building, and cried of embarrassment, shame, and desperation. Looking and smelling like a cheese ball, I wasn't about to approach a stranger for help. Of course this split personality husband of mine found me and tried approaching me, and that is when I threw my wedding rings into a field and threatened him with a large rock I picked up. I could have killed him, literally. The hatred was BOILING inside. I just sat there crying for about an hour, and my eye was completely swollen shut. All I could think about was my family and going to my kids. However, with my eye the way it was I knew if I went to my mom's, my family would NEVER accept Jerry back around, and although I wanted it to be over, I was scared. The domestic abuse cycle had left me very dependent on him, and I was under his complete manipulation.

There is a strong hold they have over us; what is that power, and why do we allow it? I am a smart woman and knew this was wrong, so why am I sitting on the side of the road, with cheese all over me and a swollen black eye, allowing this man to convince me he was sorry and actually get back in a car with him? FEAR. Fear of not getting high to numb the pain in my eye, fear of him killing me, fear of being alone, fear of facing life, fear, fear, fear. Are you faced with fear? Identifying your fears is a big step in finding a way to pull yourself up. We need to dissect the problems to be able to start mending them. Try identifying some of your fears keeping you from taking actions you know you should. Make a list and put them in order from small to biggest fears and start tackling the smallest fears first. Once you have overcome a fear, you are stronger and ready to tackle the next one, moving down the list until you conquer your biggest fear.

After this, I said to hell with it and went all out on self-destruct mode. I just didn't frickin' care if I lived or not anymore because, honestly, all I wanted was to stay high. I was trapped and felt I had no way out of this situation. He wasn't letting me leave in my car, so I was basically a hostage to him and the crack once again!

To continue maintaining our high, Jerry broke into a vehicle and stole a purse that evening. I used the identity from the purse and forged a check at a casino for $750.00. Of course, I was the one always to be on camera, not him. Jerry was upset that I had written the check for a felony amount and actually went back into the casino and tried to return the money and retrieve the check. He had his moments where he convinced me he cared about me, but this was just another form of his manipulation. At this point I knew the forged check would send me to prison so no longer cared about anything but getting high. We smoked $600.00 worth of crack within the next twenty-four hours just to hide from reality and my swollen black eye! One week later, the State Police came to our home after getting tips from running our pictures on Crime Stoppers. They literally busted our door down like you see on the show *COPS*. Holy shit! Who the hell had I become, and where is Mistie, the once strong, smart, and independent warrior? I was a professional working in all the local hospitals and now was seen with a horrible black eye plastered all over the news as "wanted." This embedded even more SHAME. Honestly, a sense of relief came over me when we were arrested because I was tired of it all. Tired of the abuse, tired of being a slave to a glass pipe, tired of running, tired of lying, tired of manipulating, tired of breaking the law, hell . . . I was just TIRED and needed sleep. I was screaming for help on the inside, but couldn't find the courage or my own voice to speak out loud.

Mom and Bill posted my $48,000.00 bond after I promised to sell our RV to repay them. Three days later I was under my mom's roof again and was happy to have her protection. I slept with my son, and we watched *High School Musical 2* as I treasured my time with my sweet li'l guy. It felt good to be by his side again, but then the intense cravings were really getting to me. I convinced myself I was okay and made the mistake of taking my car alone, against my parents' wishes, to meet my bondsman in the other town to sign papers. I stopped at our house and was thrown back with guilt about the busted doors the cops left at our rented house. They had gone through all our things, which felt like such an invasion of privacy. I'm not sure what they were looking for, but it wasn't dope because they left plenty of that laying around my house. It happened INSTANTLY without hesitation or thought—I picked up the dope on my bathroom counter and was lighting a pipe loaded with crack that quick, like my body was just going through the motions without my conscious permission. Then, once I took that first hit, I didn't stop.

My mom kept calling my cell phone, but I didn't answer due to my paranoia they could "track" me or guilt me and ruin my high. Somehow, I managed to talk to her that afternoon, and she begged in desperation for me to come home. Apparently, there was a hurricane coming through, and I was oblivious to any news of it. I saw wind and rain as I drove around smoking, but the "alarms" that would normally alert a sane person of danger were turned off. I drove right through it-an actual hurricane. I was high as a kite. I guess that is why I didn't see any dealers standing on the usual corners.

The influence of cocaine was not the only thing driving me to self-destruct or punish myself. Abuse, disappointing others, anger, shame, guilt, fear, resentment, bitterness, adultery, and another failed marriage were also driving forces. When I passed my emotional point of no return, I knew the only way I was going to be able to stop was to die, go to jail, or be found by my family who always "hunted" me down, spending hours looking for me. I had never imagined the other alternative to stop the insanity. I could have never seen this nightmare coming . . . the day IT happened. The day I'll never forget. The day my life was saved by taking the life of someone else.

CHAPTER TWELVE

SEPTEMBER 18, 2007

I ended up driving around in a town I didn't know after making random turns down dark roads, taking hit after hit. I had very little money and hadn't slept in three days. I had just bought hygiene products, food, clothes, and gas with a stolen check and needed dope to stay awake and calm the intense cravings. The night was still, nobody would sell to me because they didn't know me, and I was fading fast.

The date September 18 used to be memorable because it was my first wedding anniversary with Eric in 1987. Our anniversary was a date celebrated for ten years until our divorce. Now, thirty years later, I would have another reason to never forget the ever-nagging relentless day— a tragic accident occurred that found me isolated in a jail cell facing a forty-year sentence. I was in the wrong neighborhood, doing the wrong things, with the wrong people when it happened. A life was taken and can't be given back.

She is gone! Saying "I'm sorry" can't fix this. DEATH IS PERMANENT. What have I done? How did my life spiral so far out of control? What will happen to me now? Fear set in but couldn't overpower my heartache of knowing I was responsible. Whatever happens to me now, I must deserve.

Have you ever had the hair stand up on your arm and give you such a chill you felt like you were just hovering over your body in amazement of your situation? Have you ever fathomed the thought of losing control of your own life? Without warning or within my grasp of imagination, addiction led me down the darkest path I was afraid I'd never return from. Between Satan and cocaine, I was being choked and suffocated and felt trapped between two nonexistent worlds, like a sci-fi movie in the making. My choices and mistakes have forever changed my life, my children's lives, and another family's lives because I accidentally took the life of someone else. If only I could go back eleven years in time and realize what the first choice of snorting a line of cocaine would end with. TICK TOCK! I never intended to harm anyone, nor realized I had been driving around four days sleep deprived and constantly high. I can never return to life before this day. I'm harnessed with those memories, and she is gone *forever*. Death is permanent, and being the one who lived is a sentence all on its own. The GUILT I have felt for living has kept me in such a dark miserable place all these years. It doesn't seem fair the one doing wrong is the one still living. Being the one left behind is not easy.

Things progressed to this monumental day, and I'll never forget the sequence of events. I was out of control after bonding out of jail and going to sign the bail papers. I was desperate to stop. I drove around hitting the glass pipe of lies while crying, begging, and pleading with myself, GOD, and cocaine to let me escape this addiction. I actually stopped a policeman and asked him to help me. I told him what I had been doing and that I wanted desperately to return home to my family but couldn't stop getting high. Have you ever felt this low, out of control and desperate? I knew I wanted to stop, but physically couldn't.

The officer I flagged down was kind and compassionate. He put gas in my car and followed me straight to the police station. He did not book or charge me, even though I had just confessed to driving high. Instead, he called my parents and sat me down in an open cell and told me I was not under arrest, but if I left he would put an APB out for me driving under the influence. My stepdad was over an hour away, and as I sat there coming down (with crack and a pipe physically on me), I started to panic. The cop left for his lunch break after giving the female dispatcher a summary of what had transpired. I was an artist at manipulation and under panic mode, I convinced the lady to let me go to my car and gather some hygiene items to clean myself up before my dad arrived. I negotiated to give her my keys as security I wasn't going to drive off, but I always kept a spare key to my car on my body for emergencies. Well, guess what? I drove right out of there. I didn't care if she would radio in an APB, all I cared about was getting a hit and stopping the shame game in my head. I drove around too scared, too weak, and too enslaved to just go home.

Late the night of September 17, 2007, I saw a girl walking down the street "tweaking" and knew she could score dope for me. I asked her if she needed a ride, and of course she jumped in and asked me to take her to "trick" at a couple of houses, and in return she paid me in dope to keep me high and stay awake. The next morning I was trying to score, and the dealers I had been scoring from were either sleeping or dry (out of dope.) I ran into her again, and she flagged me down. I gave her a ride because I knew she could score for me. She got in my car and said, "My friend is doing a 'trick'" and asked me to wait for her. My heart went out for them both being on the streets prostituting at such a young age. All I wanted to do was help them, but also knew they could help me stay high, so I agreed to let her in. She scored some dope, and the three of us drove around getting high. I offered them food I had just bought, hygiene products, and makeup. I knew they were tired and I even offered to let them rest in my car for a while. My kindness only targeted me as a "duck," and they decided to rob me instead.

One of the girls got out of the car to score dope the second time, and I was totally not expecting her to do what she approached my vehicle and did next. My window was rolled down, and she showed me the dope then punched me in the face, breaking my eyeglasses and knocking them off. Meanwhile, the other girl grabbed my purse from my console and jumped out of the passenger door. I couldn't believe what was happening. Why were they doing this to me after I had been nice and helped them? This wasn't my first rodeo, but I was definitely in deeper waters than had ever been in before and knew I was in grave danger.

My first responses were ANGER, SHOCK, and RAGE. I sped away, turned around, and headed right towards them as this was the only way out of there I knew. I would have *never* hit them, but I wanted to scare them like they did me. As I turned the corner making the block trying to find my way out of a "hood" I wasn't familiar with, fear was choking me. Lost in the labyrinth of manipulation, games, and danger, I rounded the corner and saw their pimp (so I assumed) running toward me. My heart was racing out of my chest, and I knew my worst fears were a reality. I had no other alternative but to speed right past them to get out of there. I was downright angry, feeling used and dispensable. Why couldn't I even get two prostitutes smoking crack to like and value me? Why were they doing this to me after all I helped them with?

As I sped by, one of them threw a brick right at the driver side window. My heart was pounding even faster, and I frantically swerved to avoid impact and lost control of my car. I was sliding sideways down the road unable to steer. I remember thinking this was it; I finally managed to let the drug win at taking my life. My altered but instantly alert brain calculated I wasn't going to avoid the collision with the tree and parked vehicle in front of the house I was quickly approaching. My life started flashing by in slow motion. This was it. I was going to die! In shock, I passed out. A woman was standing in her yard near the parked vehicle smoking a cigarette. I never saw her, and I couldn't have stopped from sliding if I had. I ran into the back corner of the vehicle sending it into a spin when it struck her and knocked her completely underneath the house, killing her. The vehicle spun around and hit my car, slamming me into the tree. Who could have ever predicted this freak accident? I apparently came to but was unaware I'd hit anything other than the tree. I was still numb from the cocaine, so felt no pain and just wanted out of that neighborhood. All I thought at that moment was *I need to get home to my kids.*

A woman ran to my window and said, "You can't leave." I told her I was okay and just wanted to go home. She said, "Honey, look at your car." When I looked out the window and saw the large dent and steam coming from the engine, I passed out again. I have no recollection of putting the car into park or turning off the engine. The next memory I have is waking up on a gurney in the emergency room and my mother staring down at me with huge tears falling from her eyes.

"Momma, I'm okay. Let's go home and see Austin."

She said, "You can't leave, baby," and that is when I lifted my arms to hug her and felt the cold angry steel wrapped around my wrist handcuffing me to the stubborn gurney. "Why am I under arrest?"

"Don't you know?" she responded.

What is happening? They must have found dope or a pipe in my car and arrested me.

My mom looked back at a detective. "Can I tell her?"

Wait. "Tell me what?" I know something is very wrong now because I see Bill crying in the shadows of the corner.

Momma leans down with a whimpering most unforgettable voice . . . "You killed someone in a wreck, baby."

Those words are ringing so loud in my pounding head that I just scream, "NO, those girls weren't in my car." My poor momma is fighting back her emotions now as she explains a lady was standing by the parked vehicle I hit. Instantly I'm pleading. . . . "I was attacked, it was an accident . . . please, God NO!!!!" With every sob I feel the air leaving my body, along with the cocaine, and I am left a hollow shell without identity, reason, or purpose. Why the hell am I alive? Why didn't I die? I lie limp and lifeless sinking into the gurney mattress as if being engulfed by defeat.

This was my rock bottom moment. Please learn from it.

STOP! Listen to me. You have no idea the feeling of taking someone's life; it is gut-wrenching pain. Honestly, I didn't understand or totally comprehend it all as I had been up for four days straight and in and out of consciousness. I just couldn't believe it was real. I was in shock and felt I was on borrowed time. I felt guilty for being alive, not knowing if I even wanted to live or how to live anymore without the cocaine coursing through my veins. I should have been the one who died, not her.

My mom leaned down to hug me, then the officer told them they had to leave the hospital because I was in custody. They only allowed them to stay until I came to and my tests showed no major injuries. I have never forgotten the defeated look in my mom's eyes as she was forced to leave her baby girl lying there crying and sobbing uncontrollably after being told I had killed someone. It had been many years since she had seen the sparkle in her sunshine girls' eyes, but now my eyes were just void and empty. I needed her; I needed somebody. Oh, God, I was lying there all alone in fear. I didn't have my loved ones to comfort me, and I could feel my best friend slowly leaving my body too, so now I'm forced to face all of this completely alone. What went up just came crashing down and I was now forced to surrender to my destiny. Now at my rock bottom, I was defeated.

I briefly woke up dazed and looked around the hospital room hoping it was a dream, but reality set in when I saw the uniformed policeman guarding my room. Had this really happened? Did I kill someone? I was devastated, remorseful, and in shock. I needed a hug from my momma—from anyone—just to ease my pain. I was grieving and scared of what was to come. Reality was beginning to set in, but I was still in a daze. Why didn't I die? My life was spared yet again.

A few hours later I was taken to the small parish jail where I gave a voluntary police statement, somehow hoping for redemption. The officer was extremely nice and nonjudgmental as he took his time with me allowing me to spew all kinds of emotional vomit his way. I couldn't wait to confess all my sins, hoping in some way this would rectify things. He obviously saw my remorse and had pity on me. He assured me the girls were in custody and were being charged with battery and theft. Somehow those charges never came about, and they were only being held in custody on old prostitution warrants. Apparently, these two girls didn't have the best reputation in town and this was their "MO" (routine.) I was angry, scared, and confused.

We never know what is around the corner. TIME is so precious and is something we can never get back. TIME away from family, TIME damaging our body, TIME in denial, TIME incarcerated, TIME self-destructing. TICK TOCK . . . What was I running from? Now I had plenty of TIME to figure it all out.

A crazy twist in my story happened when my jail cell opened up in the middle of the night and a lady fell into the bed next to me. I got up and gave her a t-shirt and some food, and we stayed up a couple of hours talking. She was sad about her lover dying. She confided in me (a stranger) about her lover being terminally ill with cancer and was so miserable she had attempted suicide a few times before she was killed. I just sat and listened to her, not knowing *who she was*. The next morning when we met in general population for breakfast, everyone was pointing fingers at us and whispering. We looked at each other like we were supposed to fight or something. Finally, somebody told us that I was the person that killed her lover. We looked at each other and all we could do was hug. God put her in my cell in the middle of the night so there would be no prejudgment and we could talk-woman to woman as strangers. I learned about the cancer and suicide attempts, and she learned it wasn't a bad drug deal retaliation but an unfortunate accident. *We both needed to know the truth* and God provided the stage for the truth to emerge.

I had gone months without counseling, depression medication, or a visit allowed from my family. I needed something positive to cling to and I tried calming my own grief and sorrow by convincing myself there was a silver lining in this situation. I was taught if we commit suicide, we don't go to heaven and by me accidentally taking her life, I saved her soul. She was no longer in pain and her death would save my life. I always knew it would take something tragic to either end my insane drug addiction or take my life. I clung to the only silver lining I could find at the time, and this is what got me through day after day. I know my life was spared (for a second time), and if I ever returned to the dark side ever again, I would endure the wrath of God. I vowed her death to be meaningful to turn my life around and desperately try to reach other addicts with my testimony in hopes of helping them before other tragedies occur. Don't let your life get away from you and end up with actions that are non-retractable. You never know what is just around the corner or on the next page in your book of life.

I will never forget what I have done, but try and find all positive angles from her death to help others, as well as myself. I've never seen a picture of her, nor could I handle seeing one, but I hope she will somehow in some weird TWIST OF FATE be an angel looking down on me and give me strength to help others. I haven't touched cocaine since that day. I never knew my last hit of cocaine would be the cause to take her last breath.

Her children have lost their momma, but my kids have gotten theirs back. I wanted so badly to reach out to her family and even wrote the poem "Changes" and a letter to her mother but wasn't allowed to pass it to them until my plea date, October 27, 2008, in fear it could be construed as harassment.

My prosecutor had gotten wind of my book and actually sat with me and skimmed some it and said, "You don't belong here, Mistie." I replied,

"Yes I do. I KILLED SOMEONE." He proceeded to explain he knew this wasn't me and I was caught up in the addiction. He promised to get me help, and he actually played a hand in getting my sentence reduced. I accepted a plea down to negligent homicide which carries a sentence of zero to five years. I got a split sentence of four years hard labor to be followed by five years probation running concurrent with my parole. After getting credit for time already served, I was left with a two-year sentence. I successfully completed the sentence and received a first offender's pardon from the state. I was blessed with the reduced sentence. I believe God was already preparing me for THIS purpose of sharing to make an IMPACT on others.

The eyewitness who saw the assault helped my case because the assault was why I lost control of my car. I am in no way shifting blame—I should not have been there doing what I was doing, but I recognize my blessing of the reduced charge. The fourteen months in a nerve-wracking, depressing, and inconsistently run parish jail took its toll on me. I was in prison October 2008 and was due to go to the parole board on January 17, 2009. However, DOC did not calculate my time until February so I missed my hearing. The parole board sent me a letter stating the next available parole hearing wasn't until May, and my release date of July 22, 2009 was within 90 days so I was DENIED a hearing. Amber was graduating in May and I felt cheated out of my parole hearing. I have told myself everything happens for a reason and God is in control, but I am learning patience is needed. I realized even a July release date was a blessing, and I had an opportunity to go home after twenty-two months!

I stayed strong and utilized my time by taking opportunities to complete classes in parenting, anger management, and substance abuse. Additionally, I tutored for the GED program and spent my time helping others. It felt good to pay the consequences and with each day I felt a little more guilt being lifted from my heavily burdened heart. I was anxious to return to being a mom again and vowed never take that for granted. I painfully regret it took this event to wake me up and let me start my journey of pulling myself up from my rock bottom. God forgive me and instill through me the power and courage to help others. I want to IMPACT you to the point you take action and start whatever healing you need to overcome your worst to live your best.

CHAPTER THIRTEEN

NEVER SAY NEVER

"ONE day you will be on your knees doing whatever it takes for dope" were the words I surprisingly heard my daddy say when I was in my first rehab. I couldn't believe he was so blunt. We didn't usually speak to each other like that, and I was offended. "No way!" I exclaimed in shock, "Daddy, that will never happen to me. I'm not like that" was my rebuttal. Apparently, my family had done their research on the drug that kidnapped their daughter and had her held hostage. I wish I had not only listened but HEARD the warnings.

While attending group therapy in 2000 at my first rehab, I heard women give their life stories, which included pornography, prostitution, being pimped at age twelve, forced to have sex with brothers, fathers, and cousins, and being forced to work to support their mate's habit. They spoke about their parents giving them their first drug or doing drugs with their family. I sat there and thought to myself, "I came from a calm middle-class family with no drug abuse, lived in a big brick house with a swimming pool, had a college education, and was close to my family." How was I supposed to stand up there and complain to them? I told my counselor the girls probably wouldn't even believe me and say I was just a rich white girl wanting attention. She told me to just start writing my life history, and I would be surprised at what might come out. I was skeptical and afraid but did it anyway. As I wrote, the dysfunction started pouring out, and I realized my life WASN'T as great as I thought it had been.

As the words formed on the paper, I remembered being sexually molested in second grade and one of my dad's employees luring me into a building, sitting me on his knee, and trying to get into my panties in fifth grade. Other issues poured onto the paper, like me having agonizing pain about abortion and my failed marriages. I had buried these truths I didn't want to accept and found cocaine to take care of numbing the pain for years. As my emotions were stirring, I became angry, resentful, and surprised at how much pain I was harboring. I had become immune to the uncomfortable memories by staying high as much as possible. Finally, I was starting to realize what the driving force was behind WANTING to stay numb.

I am in no way justifying an addiction to help cope with a life that wasn't perfect. Remember, what goes up must come down, and after the high wears off, all the same baggage is present, but NOW WE ARE SO MUCH MORE—we are addicts too. When we hear someone speak of a situation they are going through, we shouldn't judge them or say "I'd never do that" or "That won't ever happen to me." The truth is, we don't know how we would react until we are in those shoes ourselves. If we were all a bit more kind and compassionate to each other we could open a gate for communication to take place, and true change may evolve. We should all strive to JUDGE less and MENTOR more. Education is the key to progress.

I had a college study partner who was in a domestic abuse situation, and I could never understand why she stayed with him. Eric and I went to her rescue a few times in the middle of the night, and I got angry at her and preached, "How can you let your husband hit you?" I knew I would never let a man do that to me and also knew "that wasn't love." I spoke too soon because I later fell into a dangerously abusive relationship and went back to the same toxic environment time and time again. NEVER SAY NEVER! If I had actively listened to my college friend and tried to understand her situation instead of judging her for staying, I could have gained her trust and maybe one day helped her get out. Additionally, had

I listened, I would have had the knowledge and experience to deal with abuse when I found myself in the same situation.

You may never find yourself in a tough situation, but be open-minded; the day may come, and don't say you would never do something. Although I was able to hold onto my dignity, self-respect and morals for many years, my addiction progressed and the sordid life I was trapped in thrusted me into a new life I was no way prepared for. My morals soon became nonexistent, and I found myself doing the things I said I'd never do. I was out of my element and didn't even blink an eye if it provided me with my next hit.

I remember the exact day I traded a sexual favor for dope. One of my dealers had been asking me for months but I told him no, I wasn't a whore and didn't do that. He was cute and charming, so when I crossed the line and finally gave in, it seemed justified as us just hooking up and the dope was merely a bonus. People trade sex all the time for what they want, right? Some girls sleep with a man because he buys them purses, shoes, or clothes. Some stay in relationships and give into sex to get their bills paid. Our warped brains will twist things to justify our behaviors because we don't want to call it flat-out prostitution. After I came down, I cried because I knew I had just crossed the line I said I'd never cross.

My career provided plenty of money, but as my addiction worsened, my job was gone, and the money ran out. I pawned golf clubs, my kid's video games, movies, TVs, two wedding ring sets, and anything else of value. I rented my cars out to dealers, traded food, and cleaned their houses for dope. I realized trading sex was much easier and faster, and since I had already crossed the line, I gave in to the faster way to get high so I wouldn't be present in my pain. As my addiction progressed, my willingness to support my high also progressed, and I did unthinkable things that still haunt me today. The progression into the darkest side of addiction is not *honestly* talked about in rehab, but should be the danger sign used to make us realize we are not protected. Why is the truth so taboo? Addiction progresses—I don't care who you are or where you come from—you are not immune; NOBODY IS! Eventually, it will happen to you as well. I thank God for my imprisonment, which kept me away long enough to have a fighting chance to end my relationship with cocaine without the physical cravings present to interfere with our breakup. I am sure I would have one day ended up homeless walking the streets all strung out due to the true enslavement to that damn glass pipe.

While I was in rehab, women warned me of my upcoming destiny, but I thought I was different and refused to believe I could ever turn into the type of person they were calling a "crack head." I have since been tormented by shame, guilt, and agonizing grief but have fought a hard fight and slowly evolved into a winner, beating the statistics. I was told I had a 3 % chance of beating cocaine addiction and due to my own stubbornness, I was determined to be a winner out of sheer competitiveness. However, a competitive drive is never enough to beat those odds. Unfortunately, it took so much more. Don't wait until you have passed the point of no return; start climbing your way out now.

Guilt and shame kept me in such a dreadfully dark, lonely, and dangerous place. I put myself in HELL with one stupid decision to snort a line of cocaine and repeatedly and wholeheartedly begged God to rescue me ever since. Although I'm grateful for my rescue, I regret it took someone dying to release me from the relentless addiction. I pray it won't have to be so traumatic for others because being the one that lives is hard. I am left behind to feel guilty for living, left behind to try and deal with my actions, left behind to face the world without her in it, left behind to remember, left behind to forgive myself, just left behind! It has been dreadful, but to live I knew I had to find a silver lining to focus on and cling to. I now realize I was "left behind" to WARN others what is to come from their addiction, "left behind" to be living testimony you CAN pull yourself up, "left behind" to be a better mom, "left behind" to share my story with honesty in hopes of making an impact, "left behind" to prove there is life on the other side of adversity, "left behind" to live better, serve others, and BE MORE. What legacy will your life leave behind? If it isn't something you can be proud of, take steps and initiate action to rewrite your future and change your story.

—— CHAPTER FOURTEEN ——

REGRETS

I have one thousand regrets for all the pain I've caused my family. I harbor regrets over my abortions, stealing from innocent people, pawning my things, hurting my kids, and everything in between. Dealing with an unexpected pregnancy seems so easy to "fix," but reality is, afterwards we are left to deal with so much emotional damage, guilt, shame, and anger. Oftentimes, we never actually deal with any of it, and it gets stuffed deeper and deeper under a layer of protection to avoid confronting our problems. After my first abortion, I continued burying my pain without ever getting closure, resolution, counseling, or forgiveness. Afterwards, I thought each one became easier to have done, but reality is I only stuffed those emotions deeper inside and numbed the memory and pain with more and more cocaine. Had I dealt with the aftermath and post-traumatic stress first, I probably wouldn't have chosen to have future abortions or had immense cravings to numb the pain of the previous one.

After Austin was born, Jerry and I relapsed, and I eventually ended up pregnant, but we were full-speed ahead on a self-destruct mission. We knew bringing another life into the world would not be the thing to do, so I scheduled an appointment to see a doctor. Addiction causes us to justify our actions so we can bear the existence of our wrongdoing. Insanity is a by-product of addiction, and one example of my insanity was being scheduled for an abortion but not being able to physically stop smoking crack long enough to drive to the doctor's office and have it done. Although I had temporarily escaped reality, my brain knew I was about to have an abortion and kept me from experiencing it sober. Honestly, the fear of facing my parents and telling them I was pregnant with Jerry's second child was greater than my own fear. I felt I constantly had to please them, and sometimes felt I couldn't even talk to them about things that were really going on in my life because their love for me ignited scolding and judgment. I guess I felt it was easier to "fix" the problem instead of facing my family. I think that is awful and don't agree with some of their methods or thoughts. My mom cried, "What if Lauren or Amber were pregnant from a violent man you knew was not good for them?" Well if they were, I definitely wouldn't try to manipulate, guilt, or force them to get an abortion. Those decisions shouldn't be made by other people, but I understood the desperation of my family to get me away from Jerry.

Although abortion offers an easy way out, the emotional damage causes many problems and is linked to increased metal health illnesses. I believe I would tell my daughters it is their decision and let them know I was there for them whatever they decide. I can only say this from a nonjudgmental place because I have lived through having to make those decisions and act on them. People who judge us for abortion probably haven't walked in those shoes. Never say never unless you have been down the same path. I have had nightmares my aborted baby was cut up and sold for parts on the black market. I was traumatized and in mourning while continuing to stifle the pain. Of course, I would soon relapse from all the unattended feelings of guilt, shame, and pain and even disgrace I felt towards myself. Nobody could ever chastise me for abortion more than I chastise myself. The heartache is unbearable, even after the counseling and healing, the pain still resonates throughout my body.

I couldn't stop getting high and missed and rescheduled the appointment two times before finally making it there. Because I was pregnant, I would throw up with every hit because my body was rejecting the toxic drug. Although I wasn't enjoying the high anymore and was zoned out mentally with guilt, my body was physically enslaved to it. I knew I was aborting the fetus, so didn't care about getting high. This is SICK! What the hell drives us to do such horrific things? ADDICTION, that's what does it. What can lift us out of this madness, and *how* the hell did I get away from such a powerful addiction? Somebody had to die to get me away long enough to detach the chains of darkness. I truly believe I would have died myself had I not gone to prison when I did. With all the chances I took and the situations I put myself in, how was I so lucky to be protected from harm out there? I can only speculate God was protecting me because HE wanted me to be a voice to help others—a voice of courage and truth, to share my RAW TRUTH.

When I say I was a slave to my addiction, I mean it in the most literal sense. Can you understand not being able to stop getting high long enough to go get an abortion? No, well keep doing your drug, and it will own you and your soul one day and you'll find yourself doing plenty of things you said you never would. I guarantee your success of staying an addict if you don't heed this warning. But don't take my word for it, look up the statistics yourself! It is never too late to get help and confront your pain. Stop hiding from it by ignoring it. Find the courage to do the work necessary to go to combat with the skeletons in your closet. What are you enslaved to? What are you hiding that is keeping you sick and depressed? Summons the courage to find out.

The legalization of abortion in 1973 via the U.S. Supreme Court's *Roe vs. Wade* ruling gave many women choices. There are plenty of Planned Parenthood programs to help you choose to keep, give up for adoption, or abort your child. If we choose abortion, we are left with our own internal guilt and criticizing judgment from others. I feel counseling should be REQUIRED after undergoing such a traumatic event, which we could no way prepare for beforehand. Most studies show abortion is linked to increased mental illness, which more times than not, goes untreated. The hardest part for me is to FORGIVE MYSELF! I believe counseling is the key to healing and have found support through ARCs (Abortion Recovery Centers) designed to help those whose decisions may have resulted in extensive difficulties coping with life. These centers can be found via a Christian-based support group at www.saveone.org. The Save One chapters are incorporated throughout some two hundred churches thus far and provide exclusive classes regarding abortion that give women the ability to share with others their feelings of remorse, anguish, and shame. These groups provide invaluable therapy, which induces self-forgiveness.

According to Discovery Series "When the Pain Won't Go Away," post-abortion feelings and experiences include:

Anxiety	Desire to replace baby
Anger	Broken/abusive relationships
Eating disorders	Betrayal
Bitterness	Flashbacks
Depression	Distrust
Grief	Guilt
Nightmares	Helplessness
Sexual dysfunction	Remorse
Substance abuse	Resentment
Suicide	Shame
Low self-esteem	Crying jags
Self-destructive behavior	Bonding problems

If five or more of the above apply to you, Post Abortion Trauma (PAT) could be indicated. To seek help coping with PAT, the following agencies are available:

America's Pregnancy Hotline 1–888–4-OPTIONS
www.thehelpline.org 1–800–672–2296
Option Line 1–800–395-HELP www.optionline.org
www.afterabortion.org www.healinghearts.org

We must remind ourselves "All sins are equal at the foot of the cross" (James 5:16), and we should help each other, not judge or ridicule. Again, my motto is "JUDGE less, MENTOR more." If each of us would only allow empathy to replace negativity, the world could truly change. Post-abortion wounds are already hard to heal because we internalize the pain and burden and continually beat ourselves up over the decision to go through with it. I encourage you to lay down your burden to God or your higher power of belief and rely on others for support. Trying to stuff these issues under layers of pain and regret only make deeper roots for emotional issues to blossom later.

By equipping ourselves with healthy tools today, we will be able to cope with all the feelings that will most likely resurface at different times in the future. Satan will taunt us back under his control by using self-doubt, guilt, and shame. We must practice forgiveness *daily*. Wake up every morning and tell yourself you love yourself. Find something, even one small thing, to love about yourself and believe it! It may be as simple as looking in the mirror and saying out loud that you like your hair, your smile, your humor, your fingernail polish, and so on. Whatever it is, LOVE YOURSELF for it and own it all day long. Rinse and repeat every day for optimal results.

If you find yourself crying right now it's because you identify with and relate to this chapter. Grab your phone NOW and call one of the numbers listed and let your healing start TODAY. The only way to pull yourself up is to start climbing, and this is one step up, so why not let today be the day? It will be a long battle, but I believe the harder we work at something, the more valuable it becomes to us.

Recovery is extremely important to me, and I place high value on the need for true recovery inside and out. Even after twelve years clean, I struggle with other issues in my life such as food addiction, stress eating, and feeling inadequate when things don't go the way I think they should. I oftentimes put high expectations on those around me and tend to overwhelm myself constantly. I've been told this is a defense mechanism I use to prevent myself from having to deal with my inner demons. If I'm busy and doing for others, I don't have to slow down and "do" for me. In order to be the best me I can and help others, I must deal with all my cobwebs on the inside first. For the last twelve years I have been slowly doing just that. I am still a work in progress but believe I have insight to help others struggling with any type of addiction, self-forgiveness, or trying to gain self-esteem after being in an abusive relationship, addiction, or depression.

Many people suffer from all kinds of loneliness: physical, mental, or even spiritual loneliness. I'm amazed at how I can be surrounded with loved ones yet feel so miserably alone like they didn't really know me at all. How many times have you sat in a room full of people yet felt isolated? Have you ever been sociable one day, then the next day feel you don't fit in or just don't feel like expending the energy to have a conversation with someone? During my addiction I was trying to fit in where I could get in. The problem was I didn't fit in anywhere. I didn't fit in with my college friends because I was now a druggie, I didn't fit in the drug scene because I was college educated, and I certainly didn't fit in jail. People always thought I was a "duck"(easy target) because I had money and was naïve about the game people run on each other on the streets. Every day out there I witnessed total manipulation to get money or dope to stay high. The dope scene is cruel and fake; nobody has true friends, only co-conspirators!

When I relapsed, I always had to leave home because my family or friends didn't use drugs, so I ran to the streets. I hated getting high alone, so I would welcome anyone to get high at my expense just to be my "friend." I was searching for some type of loyalty from ANYBODY! I was isolated and lonely, stuck in-between both worlds, still feeling unaccepted by either. It was a sad and dark place.

How can we be surrounded by loved ones, children and friends yet feel so isolated and alone? I spent ten years in addiction a lonely woman and a complete stranger to my reflection in the mirror. At times I could appear to have it all together and present so strong, but I was crying and shaking on the inside. Satan stole my identity during domestic abuse and addiction, so I found myself wondering what my favorite foods, colors, and music were. I spent so long trying to fit in that I lost my originality and identity in the process. I walked around taking up physical space without meaning or purpose. Still today, the core of most of my pain comes from being locked away from my kids and putting them through so much hell during those dark years. The regretted decisions are astronomical, yet permanent. The hardest part of doing time for me was not seeing them, touching them, or putting my arms around them at all. Some ask, "How can you say you love and miss your kids, yet run off for days at a time?" Well, that is the power of addiction. I always had the security of knowing my parents or husband were there to tend to them, and while I wonder if

I hadn't had that safety net, if I would have still done it. The chances are, yes! Addiction wins over everything else. GET UP and FIGHT for your life, you are worth it!

During incarceration, others in my life endured pain as well. My kids, parents, and any friends I had left all missed the old Mistie. I heard many girls in jail talk about the state taking custody of their kids or abandoning them permanently and leaving them to be raised by family members. They would cry and say how much they missed them, yet as soon as they were released they met their dealer before seeing their kids and oftentimes would be back in jail before ever making it to see them. Instead of being judgmental, I came to understand the power of addiction and the hold it can have over us. I believe it is even more than a decision; it is a trained mindset of not feeling worthy. After having timespans without using, I would be level-headed, without the mind-altering substance, yet still make a conscious decision to relapse. There was something broken or missing inside, and my mindset was to fill the void or avoid the pain. I regret not realizing I needed to identify the source sooner, before I damaged myself and the relationships around me.

Loneliness in jail was almost unbearable. I longed for a hug from someone or a simple shoulder to cry on. I was strong for so many of the young girls in there and became someone for them to lean on. However, I searched for someone to have compassion for me that I could lean on. Then, guilt and anger set in because I was giving girls advice I should have been giving to MY kids. Mentally, I would beat myself up thinking I'd lost my chance with my girls because while incarcerated they were twenty and seventeen. Now, I realize our kids need us no matter their age. Poor little Austin was only seven when I went to prison and he was extremely lonely for MY touch and comfort. He would cry on the phone and beg me to come get him. My mom, thinking she was doing best for him, refused to let me tell him where I was and that I *couldn't* come home. He spent two years thinking I was away in a hospital getting better from a wreck. I hated lying to him but didn't have a choice except to follow my mom's wishes during this time. I carried so much anger over this and am still working through the resentment. However, what I grew to realize was I put myself in that position, and it was my fault, not my mom's. She was completely altering her life to take care of him in my absence. Account-ability for me was a big part of recovery and being able to pull myself up. Once I stopped blaming others for all my mistakes, I started realizing how much devastation *my* addiction had brought down on my loved ones around me. Step up and own up.

Unfortunately, once I understood this, SELF-FORGIVENESS was ahead of me, and that alone is such a mentally abusive mind game. On top of that, I had fears of letting myself, my family, and loved ones down again. I knew in my heart I couldn't ever touch drugs again after taking somebody's life but also struggled knowing the hold the drug had over me. I was scared, lonely, and anxious. My life has been spared in two wrecks, and I finally understand what it means to "fear God." I fear the consequences and wrath if I were to ever return to drugs. Therefore, I have vowed to make my victim's death be the wake-up call to save my life and hopefully, through my testimony, save others. I am a life shifter now, teaching others to honor their regrets and come to terms with them I teach my four step method, C.O.P.E. (confront, optimize, push through, and embrace the past) and share my experiences with authority to help others. *If I can, you can.* I am living to C.O.P.E., will you?

─── CHAPTER FIFTEEN ───

C. O. P. E.

C oping with everything I have gone through has been a hard task, and I realize it will be a never-ending journey requiring lifelong maintenance. We must constantly take inventory of our mental and physical health and do an attitude check as well. The true key to being able to love ourselves is doing the work required to get closure on the things haunting us so we can close a chapter to allow a new exciting chapter to begin. Therefore, the faster we get to work, the sooner our new life starts. My C.O.P.E. method is a perfect starting point for this self-renewal journey. C.O.P.E. = HOPE! These four steps are simple to follow, but require you to spend time with each one, carefully adhering to the focus of the action. Grab some paper and let's get to work right now.

C—CONFRONT—Confront your fears and memories haunting you by *physically* writing them down one at a time on a piece of paper in detail. Just start writing, and I promise the pain and resentment will come out through your words. The list may be longer than you anticipated as the writing will spark things that may be suppressed and will surface as you make your list. This is for you, and you only, so don't worry about form or spelling. Spend some time (it took me three days) to complete your list and number each item. This is an example of how I got started:

1. I am angry my incarceration kept me from both my daughters' high school graduations.
2. I resent Jerry had physical control over me, and resent Austin had to witness him hit me.
3. I feel shameful for the abortions I've had.

Keep your list going and include as many items as you can because identifying the pain is an important first step. Once you complete your list, burn, flush or shred it. Do whatever you can to release it *from* you. Once you've released it, start living for your future. You survived it, so you have won. Embark on a new journey to become a better version of you by making healthier choices moving forward. Get out of the rearview mirror, smash the gas pedal, and enjoy the exciting road ahead.

O—OPTIMIZE—Optimize from your experiences and realize you are an authority on them now that you have lived through them. Find the educational life lesson part of your situation and optimize what you can learn from it. I used to be judgmental and a bit arrogant until I lived through things myself, realizing we have no idea how we would react until we are in the same situation (Never say never.) Start a list showing things you can optimize on. An example would be:

1. I used to think my husband cheated on me because I wasn't pretty enough, a good enough sex partner, or fun enough for him. I now realize the defect was in him, not me. He cheated due to his own hang-ups of needing to feel adequate or important. Now, I can help others understand they can't equate THEIR worth based upon others' actions. My sharing the experience of surviving will help other's not carry guilt of a failed marriage they weren't solely responsible for.
2. I used to think "JUST SAY NO" to the drink, drug, food, gambling, and so on. Now living through ten hellacious years of

addiction and still battling a food addiction, I realize it isn't such a simple task. There is an incredible power struggle taking place inside your brain for the "*you*" wanting help and the "*you*" wanting to run from the help. Now I understand all too well what a struggle it is to say no, stop, or not act on impulse to run from reality. I teach how to use the energy on ourselves and strive to be a better, healthier person moving forward.

Start your list and you will realize how many things you have become an authority on now. If you choose to ACT and cause a reACTION, you can be a powerful resource to others going through similar things.

P—PUSH THROUGH—This is where it gets a little harder because Satan, your negative voice, or whoever, does not want you to succeed and will use anything possible to prevent this step. Writing stuff down on paper was easy, but to actually let go of all of it is challenging. I got stuck here for a long time (weeks) because my heart was telling me to forgive others and forgive myself, but my mind was saying, hell no. I wanted to hang on to the pain because it somehow validated who I thought I was. I played tug-of-war with myself trying to push through these emotions. It took effort to heal myself and actually BELIEVE I was worth it, realizing we are a better version of ourselves when healthy instead of housing a toxic heart filled with anger and resentment. The most helpful reasoning for me to accomplish this step was to ask myself, "How can I ask someone to forgive me for my wrongdoings, but then not forgive someone else?" Go back to the list you made when confronting your demons in step 1 and start one by one forgiving either yourself or the person accountable for the wrongdoing. Tell yourself "I forgive you so I can be forgiven too." Here are a couple of examples of how I was able to push through:

1. Instead of carrying resentment about Eric being an alcoholic, running off with his mistress, and blaming him for never paying child support, I find the positive in the situation and am thankful he was physically there for our girls when I was absent later in life. He might have done things I didn't agree with, but he kept our girls

safe, had strict curfews and rules with them, and provided a stable environment. I thank him for stepping up when I was in "runaway mom" mode. By focusing on the positives, I no longer dwell on the negatives. Those times have passed anyway, so why not let it go? DO NOT ALLOW YOUR PAST TO ROB YOU OF YOUR FUTURE!

2. Instead of beating myself to death emotionally about taking someone's life, I focused on how she was suicidal with terminal cancer and cling to the silver lining that I saved her soul, which in turn saved my life. It was an orchestrated ballet of events that led to the ultimate rock bottom for me, but look what has come from it: my kids have their mom, and she is no longer suffering and suicidal. This attitude allowed me to push through the guilt for being the one that lived that day!

E—EMBRACE—Once you have confronted, optimized, and pushed through, turn around and embrace your life. Know you have survived and are a VICTOR WITH AUTHORITY. Stop hiding your skeletons in the closet; instead, let them out to dance around and show others they aren't so scary after all! You are unique in your experiences and outcomes, hand-picked to survive so you can stand tall and own your voice of truth. Are you going to waste your knowledge and victories, or teach others how to be survivors too? If you keep it all to yourself out of fear, shame, or guilt, you are being extremely selfish. Haven't you been through something only wishing you could identify with someone else going through the same thing? Without owning your life, good and bad, others will never know they aren't alone. An example of me embracing my past is:

1. Realizing how telling the *real* truth about cocaine leading me to do things I said I would never do for my next high has opened a door for other people to feel comfortable opening up about their truth too. By releasing the truth, other people trust me and feel they can share in honesty and *really* talk with me. In turn, this gives them hope for a bright future as I'm living proof that a life can be rebuilt after addiction and adversity.

2. I have embraced having multiple felonies that will always be attached to my name. I went through all of it and endured the pain to come out gaining HUMILITY. I have a completely different view of life now, having existed in different dimensions of reality, and those felonies are how I have gained the knowledge to fill my pages with words of hope. Additionally, the time I spent incarcerated gave me a new value on life, and the one thing we can never rewind, get more of, or stop is TIME.

I know after you complete my C.O.P.E. method you will feel renewed and powerful. I have come to realize all the stuff I've been hiding has given me power to make a difference in other people and their world. The power of giving is a feeling I never understood before, but after witnessing it, I am determined to help you achieve the same joy.

—— CHAPTER SIXTEEN ——

REFLECTION

Hindsight is 20/20.

I gradually worked on my insecurities and was determined to make my incarceration time productive by putting in some hard work to heal ME. Being locked down allowed enough time to lapse to ride through the cravings and get to a point I could re-learn to live without cocaine coursing through my veins. Also, once away from the abusive situation, I started realizing how toxic and damaging the domestic abuse left me. I was completely stripped of my identity. I no longer knew what *my* favorite food or music was because those things were dictated by my abuser. It was empowering to watch my own preferences emerge timidly one at a time. Due to the brainwashing, manipulating, and control, I never saw the abuse for face value. I either justified or denied the truth out of avoidance of facing the underlying issues. I perceived Jerry checking Wal-Mart and gas receipts as his watching our budget instead of realizing he was checking times on the receipt to make sure I had come straight home. He was guilty of shenanigans, so he assumed I was too. When a spouse constantly accuses us of something, they themselves are usually the guilty one. My sister always tried to explain this to me but I was too spellbound to see the writing on the wall.

For years I have fought resistance of letting go of my anger and resentment over my powerlessness. Once I learned to stop being the victim and start being the authority, I began speaking my mind, voicing my opinion, and feeling comfortable enough to get angry without fear of being ridiculed or scared of a broken nose. I learned I can sit in a room full of people and not feel lonely or isolated anymore and now have confidence to engage in conversation and actually feel others find me interesting, smart, and funny. Things really turned around when I started focusing on me instead of focusing on pleasing a man, friend, family member, or boss. I shifted my focus to my three wonderful kids.

We must take ACTION to get a reACTION. When will you take your first step? I hope you C.O.P.E. as I did and allow the breakthrough from *victim* mentality. It is what it is, and we can't change any of it, but we can damn sure decide our own future. Do you have the courage to start looking on the inside to climb out of your own binding skin? Take control by utilizing my C.O.P.E. method and let go of your pain so you can show up in your future.

While incarcerated I became one hundred pounds overweight and completely miserable about my appearance, yet too lazy or depressed to do anything about it. With drug addiction, you don't eat much and typically drop weight quickly. The downfall is when you stop, you gain it back just as quickly. My metabolism was as unstable as my emotions. I made excuses and convinced myself my thyroid must be underactive and slowing my metabolism. Well, the truth is maintaining an ideal weight is simple arithmetic. To lose, we must expend more than we take in. To maintain, we eat and exercise proportionately. To gain, we eat more than we expend. Seems so simple, huh? Well in a 50-foot long, 12-foot wide room with nineteen other girls and very little room to expend energy, it is much easier to gain. We had no exercise equipment, balls, jump ropes, or any other sports-related props.

Occasionally we wrapped a toilet paper roll in a sock and played baseball using our hands as a bat and maxi pads stuck to the floor as bases. However, most of my time was spent lying in my bed either with headphones on to block out all the gossip, noise, and arguing or just sleeping out of depression. My weight blew up and just added to the low self-esteem

Jerry made sure to leave me with. It was exhausting trying to please him every day by trying to look good enough, trying to be on his time, always having to check in with him, keeping the house clean, accounting for the money I spent (even though I was the one earning it), keeping the bills current, dressing right (conservatively), or saying the right things. I lived on a constant rollercoaster where one day he would tell me I was very beautiful and he loved my hair and eyes and wanted to make love to me, then the next day he would remark I was fat and unattractive, and he rejected me sexually. Who can keep up? So, again my happiness was hinged upon someone else. Now, I wake up thankful to be alive and cherish my life, knowledge, health, eyes, hair, teeth, sense of humor, education, courage, wisdom, compassion, and feeling of love and being loved. I realize how important we must find our own happiness before striving to please someone else. I hope to keep growing and strengthening my soul.

I remember a counselor in rehab once told me an analogy that has really stuck with me and makes a lot of sense. She said to imagine the ocean and all the layers of different types of fish. As addicts and convicts, we are typically at the bottom where it is dark, and we feed off the scum and waste from the fish above. While crawling along the ocean floor, we are only in contact with other scum suckers, so we associate with and attract other bottom dwellers. As we heal on the inside and gain more self-worth, we rise up to a new level where there are better fish, better food, and healthier water. As we continue to heal, we will rise to the top of the ocean where the sun shines, the fish are beautiful tropical colors, and food is fresh. The healthy warm water is where we will start attracting other healthy mates because we are no longer in the presence of the scum at the bottom. I felt like scum during that dark and lonely decade of my life but will no longer settle for the waste on the ocean floor! I strived to float to the top before I walked out of prison to return to my family a better, healthier me. I was blessed to return to a non-drug-using family and not be tempted with relapsing due to association. Unfortunately, others return home to moms, dads, brothers, kids, or cousins and friends that are still swimming at the bottom of the ocean. The company we keep has such an influence on our own life. Although my family wasn't a trigger to relapse, their GUILT and ANGER are just as powerful, and we must protect ourselves from their uncontrollable outbursts at us. We need to be patient with those close to us and give them time to learn the new person without the addiction. I warn against allowing toxic relationships to drive you back to feeling bad about yourself. If you can't filter out their hurtful words, do not put yourself in the position to let them "vent" or attack you over the past. Kindly remind them you have survived and are no longer that person. Ask them to try and forgive you for the past and live present with you as the person you are now. This is hard, especially because we feel we owe them the chance to say what they want for putting them through so much. Consider counseling to mediate dialogue between you and them to allow them a safe place to vent their anger toward you, yet not allowing you to internalize and self-destruct over their words.

Being around people in positions we want to be will help speed our victory of becoming our better version. 1: Corinthians 15:33 says, "Bad company corrupts good character." I get angry at myself because I was not raised around any drugs or alcohol, yet voluntarily strayed to that lifestyle. Some other addicts are born into unfortunate environments and just follow suit. I would love to go on a talk show one day and say, "It wasn't my parents' or friends' fault" and just stand up and say, "I am the screw up" instead of shifting blame like many others do. If we are casting blame on anyone else for our actions, we are still in the stage of denial. We made a conscious decision to succumb to the action and then, once addicted, lost control or power to stop. Don't wait until your event happens that plummets you to rock bottom. Start looking inward and healing yourself, and eventually the void you fill with your addiction will eventually fill up with forgiveness, love, and ambition to BE MORE and possibly help others.

NA and AA meetings help many people stay away from drugs and alcohol by providing free methods proven successful utilizing a twelve-step program. However, for me personally, it kept my mindset in the drug. Hearing "war" stories for two hours about this drug, that drug, or whatever the topic just kept cocaine on my mind constantly. For others it proves therapeutic, but the meetings always left me feeling like I had gotten high or wanting to get high. Counselors told me I was suppressing my problems and justifying not attending the meetings. Regardless, I instead found my method to C.O.P.E., and it has changed my life. My way isn't the only way, so I just encourage you to find what *works for you* and stay with it long enough to let it work! Give yourself the benefit of the doubt and ride it out.

For several years I felt guilty for being the one that lived on 9/18/07 and repeatedly beat myself up from the inside out. After having a life-shifting breakthrough to change my mindset, I realized this single event could not possibly define my future. Honestly, out of everything I have lived through to date, I must admit the domestic abuse left me more scarred than anything else. The verbal abuse leaves deep scars that take years of affirmations to overcome. The physical abuse leaves physical scars as constant reminders that either embarrass or strengthen us. I have spent many hours with counselors trying to "fix" my low self-esteem, insecurities, and guilt domestic abuse left behind. It is important to find support and get the anger out in a therapeutic environment with others that understand. We lose so much identity and self- worth when abused, and to pull ourselves up, we must regain control of our lives. The physical and emotional scars will never completely heal, but I use them as a reminder of what direction I want my life to grow. Instead of self-pity, we can choose to use our life experiences in a positive way by realizing we lived through something dreadful but now have authority to speak about it. I have chosen to share my truth to shed light for someone to understand they aren't alone and aren't the monster they have convinced themselves they must be.

Abortions, seeming to be an easy "fix," only left me scarred with guilt and shame. My pain taught me to be more tolerant, sympathetic, and compassionate instead of judgmental. If we all just do our part, *we* could make a difference. If *we* judge less and mentor more, WE can start a movement. If WE show empathy and understanding, WE can shift negativity.

It takes digging deep through our flaws, hang-ups, and denials to sort all this out, but I admit feeling free and buoyant after doing so. Facing our own fears is not easy, but if we take time for ourselves and quit trying to be people pleasers, we can start to love ourselves and see the qualities and talents the Lord has blessed each of us with.

Poetry is definitely one of my outlets. I was gifted to express my feelings through poetry but had long abandoned that practice. In taking small steps to find myself, I reconnected with poetry while incarcerated and used it as an emotional outlet instead of merely just doing time. Writing is therapeutic, and our words are powerful whether written in private and locked away or shared with others. The act of writing from within heals our soul. I've written letters to my ex–husbands forgiving them, cussing them out, and asking them for forgiveness. Many letters were written only to be thrown away without being read by them. I've even written my own obituary to recognize what others may have to say about me. Writing is an effective and useful tool in any form, especially daily journaling. I encourage you to form a habit of releasing your anger onto paper by way of words.

Incarceration was hard to endure while watching time tick away, knowing it was time lost forever. Therefore, I decided to utilize my time wisely and started an exercise program in my small, dim parish jail by walking fifty laps around the metal table in the center of the room after every meal. I used a deck of cards to keep count of my laps and practiced giving myself affirmations with each lap. As I walked, endorphins were released, and I became livelier and more energetic. Over time, I felt a sense of pride and accomplishment, which motivated me to be more. Self-improvement became my new "high." It felt good to accomplish things all on my own. I have always been told how strong I am because I can go the extra mile to do for others, but when it comes to helping myself, I usually lacked the love, worth, or motivation.

Completing my sentence on parole/probation was another accomplishment I found pride in. Once I quit trying to manipulate the system and actually lived a sober life, doing probation was easy. If I had been forced to stay in jail the first time I got in trouble, without chance after chance on probation, maybe I would have learned a hard lesson from the beginning. I try and count my blessings now, not my worries. I realize there is always going to be someone worse off than me and try and help those people instead of wallowing in self-pity and complaining about what I don't have.

After living two very different lives, I have been humbled a great deal and try to learn from my mistakes and heartaches. I desperately want to reach out to someone and be heard to provide them something they can relate to instead of feeling isolated and alone in their madness and insanity. Honestly, all the words and stories in the world could never express the double life I've lived. Learning to see my glass as half-full instead of half-empty allowed me to start healing. Regardless what level our own rock bottom is, we all have to pull up to escape our hell. What will it take for you to turn your life around and let go of your past? Are you willing to do the work now to pull yourself up so you won't have to find out what your bottom is? If so, there is HOPE, and C.O.P.E. = HOPE! Again, I say find what works for you and give it your all. If you fail, ask for help and keep trying. Failure is how we gain wisdom and knowledge along the way. Ultimately, NOT giving up is what separates success from failure.

Some people speak to hear themselves talk; I want to speak and be heard because there is a difference. When I started writing this book I couldn't imagine anyone would care to read all about my sordid life. Why would anyone care? We all have our own story to tell, so what makes mine any different? I realized my life was spared after surviving two wrecks for a reason, so I set out to find the reason. I believe God would not carry me through all I survived without a purpose. It takes time to go through the healing process and learn to C.O.P.E. daily. Once I forgave myself and let go, I found STRENGTH and PURPOSE. My mission is for you to look into the once toxic mirror and see beauty and light in your reflection.

CHAPTER SEVENTEEN

MOTHERLY LOVE

A mother's love is secure, unconditional, warm, comforting, soothing, and like no other. A mother is someone no other person could replace. While in jail at age forty, I lay in bed and cried for my mom. I realized there are three children that cry for me like that too. Looking back, I just can't believe the things I did, didn't do, or didn't even try to do! I am sick over the amount of TIME wasted and want so badly for you to hear how to pull yourself up before you waste precious time as well. TICK TOCK!

Before drugs, I was a wonderful mother and very involved in my kids' lives. They had 100 percent of me, and when my escapade of self-destruction started, they barely got 25 percent. I can NEVER make up the time lost. It's gone. I've deprived them of loving memories and instead gave them memories of their mom missing birthdays, proms, first dates, and even high school graduations. They stayed confused and insecure because when I escaped the influence of cocaine for varying time spans, I would be "Super Mom" again and go out of my way to make things up to them. However, no matter how hard I tried, no present could ever replace the absence of their mother. They wanted and needed ME. I can say Lauren and Amber have gained strength from all of this and are loving, beautiful, smart, and responsible young women. Austin went through my addiction at a much younger age than the girls did, so he didn't understand as much. Instead, he is left with ANGER for me going away for two years. He has a heart the size of Texas and is full of compassion. He loves the Lord and has a charming and witty personality. I am proud of my three children as they have surpassed all odds and turned out productive, loving, and responsible young adults, despite the childhood they were dealt. God continues to bless us and I am thankful they have strength from their hardships.

Lauren displays unconditional love for me but has always voiced her anger and let me know when she was pissed or disappointed. Lauren is blunt and outspoken, in a pleasingly confident manner. She has been a great source of strength for me because she is forgiving, loving, and compassionate—qualities and values that were always noticed in me. She nurtured and protected Amber and Austin during my absences and developed strength because of it. Her attitude is, "I saw what drugs have done to all our lives, Momma, and I'm too smart to go that route." I pray she never does. She has been a survivor despite having an alcoholic dad and part-time mother on drugs. Lauren was a cheerleader and soccer goalie with talent beyond measure, but after she moved to live with her dad, she never tried out for anything at her new school. She was left insecure and lonely and didn't have the confidence then to step into her light. I feel I robbed her of a different high school memory she could have had if only I had been the mom they deserved with a stable home. However, I recognize the importance and significance that *I am there for her now*!

Lauren fell in love with Henry in eighth grade when we lived in Albuquerque. After all my shenanigans, she had to move to Texas to live with her dad and didn't see Henry for several years. They sparked a telephone romance their senior year, and after graduation he moved to Texas, and they have been together ever since. They waited many years to have a baby, then I got a call from her telling me my first grandbaby was due on—you guessed it—SEPTEMBER 18th!! Wow. God is replacing a life with the life I stole. She had a normal pregnancy and went into labor September 17, and Eliana was born on her due date of September 18. There was an oxygen deprivation and our sweet girl suffered a brain injury resulting in HIE grade 3 (Hypoxic ischemic encephalopathy.) She is blind, deaf, doesn't hold her temperature, can't suck, swallow, or cry, has a feeding tube, and many other issues. She has never heard the songs they both sing to her at night, and they have never gotten anything concrete back from her as far as saying their names or even laughing at their voices. She does recognize their scent, vibrations, and touch, and Lauren and Henry are the best parents Eliana could have. They sacrifice so much to give her all the love she deserves. She requires constant 24/7 care and was in and out of the hospital so much that Lauren had to give up her career in hotel management, but she was happy to do so for her little special girl. Again I say, Lauren is the strongest woman I know!!!!

Can you believe for the first few months of Eliana's life I actually let the devil convince me her condition was all my fault? It must be my punishment for all the wrong I had done, right? The date, *SEPTEMBER 18th,* couldn't just be a coincidence! I let all the negativity and guilt of my past keep me from feeling joy. Then, while developing my C.O.P.E. method realized my past didn't have to define my future and I said hell no! I have come too far to let my past rob me of my future. I realized everything I had gone through and drug my kids through had left them STRONG, INDE-PENDENT, AND RESILIENT. They are armored to face life head on, and that is the silver lining in their living through my addiction.

Our li'l hummingbird is three now and has her fair share of medical issues which require 24/7 care, and they face issues every day they tackle together, but I couldn't be more proud of them. They waited until Eliana had been hospital free nine months and somewhat stable before deciding to try and have another baby. Fear and emotion was high as we all awaited the birth of our li'l cub, Harper (Harper Bear.) She is perfect in every way and has brought so much joy and love to us all. Lauren and Henry teach her to love her sister and make sure they are as close as her condition allows. They teach Harper to give Eliana kisses and love on her sister very "easy." They have struggles and endure tiring and trying nights, but their family is wealthy with LOVE and RICH with compassion. Henry works hard, goes to school pursuing an engineering degree at night and takes a four hour shift when they don't have night nursing to care for their sweet girl. Lauren makes sure Eliana is clean, cared for, and keeps on top of all her needs. She has an online Etsy store (Bear and bird design) where she sells beautiful hand-crafted crochet items she creates. She spends hours crocheting to make extra money to help with the bills. I have so much respect and love for them and thankful I am now present to help and be somebody stable to lean on. Lauren and I have rebuilt a sound relationship which is growing stronger every day. It has taken her some time to call on me as she never had me there to depend on before. Now after twelve years she knows I am here to stay and I love how she calls me for advice, vents to me or leans on me. Through it all, she is proud of me and encourages me to speak out and help others. She is a blessing to all who know her.

Amber was in second grade when the insanity began and was always such a Momma's girl. Eric left when she was in first grade so she didn't have the same bond with him Lauren did. She is smart, talented, beautiful, aggressive and high spirited- qualities I remember having myself. She used her anger to fuel athletics and excelled in everything she competed in. She thought if she was the best in sports and smartest in school, I would love her enough to stop using drugs and stay home. She is a nationally ranked junior Olympic distance runner (Junior Olympic silver medalist), all stars basketball, soccer and at one time volleyball player too. She also scored perfect on her Texas TAAS exam. She is an overachiever just like me and puts tremendous pressure on herself. She would always love on me when I'd come home from a mission and say "it's okay Momma, I love you." She just wanted me home and although she was angry on the inside, she saved the anger for her sports.

Sadly, I was blinded of their pain by my high and too weak and scared to confront it. One summer Amber went to my sister's and I was told she went out in the pasture and just screamed in a rage and then cried to her cousin about what she had been going through. She even revealed she contemplated cutting her wrists with a bottle from the trash can when I was late picking her up from soccer practice one time. How selfish I had been, if only I could help myself! When I heard about this it sent me even FURTHER under a blanket of guilt and remorse and only made my addiction worse because instead of finding the root of my problems, I continued running and using the high for relief from the pain.

Amber is level-headed, practical and always see's things black and white. She doesn't get bogged down with the grey in the middle. It either is, or it isn't. I call on her for advice when I'm having trouble making a decision on something. She is extremely compassionate and one of the most UNSELFISH people I know. She stayed true to course and pursued her nursing degree, becoming a certified critical care nurse (CCRN.) She fell in love with Julie, who she is now happily married to. They are both nurses and have a loving, respectful and honest marriage and seem extremely happy. Amber is currently back in school obtaining her DNP, Doctorate Nurse Practitioner CRNA degree for Nurse Anesthetist. She is my ride or die and we are very close and have rebuilt a beautiful mother-daughter bond. I depend on her for sound, logical and practical advice quite often. She isn't my clone physically, but has all my strengths, personality and mindset.

My Li'l Man, Austin, who I thought was my "cure" from God to get off drugs, came nine years behind his sisters and never experienced the same "Super Mom" at 100 percent they did. He only experienced a part-time mom leaving for three or four days at a time on a vacation with cocaine. Of course, when I'd manage to stay away from cocaine for six months to one year at a time, we were extremely close, and I was a good mom, leaving good memories for short periods of time. I'm sure those memories only confused him more as he was too young to understand the situation.

Jerry went to prison on Father's Day when Austin was one and got out and became a part of his life at age six. He only knew Jerry Dada from visits Bill took him on at the prison. Gene was his "daddy" as far as Austin knew. He and Gene were very close, and when Gene left and hooked up with Bimbo #2, Austin was left heartbroken and further confused. Austin has fond memories of Gene, and we all thought Gene would be the one to stick around and raise him as his own, but he just pulled a "Mistie" and disappeared. Jerry got released from prison and played daddy for one-and-one-half years until he was gone again too. Austin has justified anger toward me, but we have been through counseling, and I insist we keep open communication as to build a healthy relationship. I remember when he was one-and-one-half years old: I was on a four-day mission during which time my mom (Nona) had him, and when I returned, Austin was actually mad at me for being gone. He displayed his anger by not coming into my arms or letting me hold him. Even as a young toddler, he knew to be angry at me for *abandoning him*; it is instinctual to want to belong and feel secure. Austin is definitely a momma's boy by default, but he had two loving grandpas that remained constant and active in his life.

I prayed God would send someone into our lives and be a great role model and father to Austin and thought my current husband, Neil would be that man. Unfortunately, that was not the case. Neil has been a great provider, chauffer, chaperone, and friend, but never really made the father-son bond with the loving arms around each other saying, "I love you son" kind of connection. Neil has been good for Austin in other ways such as their shared passion for music/percussion, Boy Scout events, and sharing his wisdom and knowledge of the world. Neil and I are currently separated headed into a divorce, and it will be interesting to see what "role" he assumes with Austin following our divorce. Neil tried to adopt Austin early on in our relationship, but my mom still had custody, and I just couldn't bear putting her through all of that legal stuff again. Neil blames me for that, and I guess because he wasn't "legally" his dad, he just fell into whatever role emerged. Austin loves Neil but has anger toward him as well. Austin has never had a dad to pal around with, take him fishing, hunting, or build a trusting relationship with. Neil has never truly recognized Austin as his son. He always made sure to introduce him as his stepson, which kept a wall between them. Perhaps this is my fault for not choosing a spouse that would be the dad Austin needed in his life.

Austin is a young man now at the age of eighteen, and I am so proud of him and his loving heart. He has used me to help close friends crawl out of addiction by being persistent until the friend came home from college and went to rehab. He lives by a strong *no drugs* policy, and I pray he keeps that attitude as well. During Easter break his sophomore year, his sisters and I revealed the truth to him about why I had been gone those two years. He cried and his first words were, "Momma, are you okay now?" He didn't say he was mad, or cuss me out; instead he was worried about me. He has such a sweet and compassionate heart. Austin is the kid who spent all his money the first day of Boy Scout camp buying everybody an ice cream that didn't have money because he felt bad for them. He attended Catholic school through eighth grade where he served his community as altar server for many years and has always shown respect for God. Although he still has anger, he displays love, empathy, and compassion toward everyone in his path.

My son has my daddy's charisma, whit, and love of music. He has been awarded Best Musician twice and excels on the drumline in high school. He plays goalie for his school and competitive traveling soccer teams. He has been in scouting since first grade, and his scoutmaster has been the best mentor for Austin, teaching him life lessons along the way. I am proud he was inducted into Order of the Arrow and recently made his Eagle Scout this past year. He is a two-time local winning recipient of the Daughters of American Revolution Essay Contest and has plans to become a trauma surgeon.

My kids shine even though you would expect them to be bitter and tarnished from their past. It is all a relative perspective and how we choose individually to let things affect us. We either succumb to the preconceived notion we are going to be failures, or we rise up to take a stand and apply *action* to be better. I am convinced they are strong and resilient because of what they have endured—another silver lining. They are authorities on how to survive when parents are absent physically and mentally due to drugs, alcohol, incarceration, divorce, or depression.

There have been so many things I've done to my children, and for years I carried heart ache and shame about causing them grief instead of being their comforter. Shame only kept me in a toxic state further disabling my ability to rise up to be the mom they deserve. Through my C.O.P.E. method, I rebuilt my bonds even stronger with each one of them. Today, we are all very close, and I am thankful for the second chance to step up and be the mom they were starved for. My heart breaks for all the moms who lose their kids to the state or just give up on life and abandon them all together. It seems overwhelming and impossible, but I believe all relationships can be re-established if built on a foundation of trust, honesty, transparency, and love. I have done unthinkable things to and with my kids, yet they were always loving and forgiving. For example, I remember relapsing and having Austin with me in the very back of the van. I gave him bottles of chocolate milk and Slim Jims to gnaw on and other snacks but didn't tend to him as I should have while driving around for hours getting high, blowing the smoke out the windows. I think he was fourteen months or so, and when I couldn't stop using and go home, I stopped the van and got out on my knees in a blizzard and prayed for strength. I cried uncontrollably, cursing the devil for having such a hold over me. When I got back in the van, I was still crying, and a sweet little voice came from the back of the van: "I sorry Momma, I sorry." There he was, a tiny baby, comforting and consoling me! How would I ever allow things to get so out of hand? Can you even imagine or fathom me doing such things? I did them, and every addict is headed in the same direction too if they don't pull themselves out of the hell they are in. My heart aches over these incidents, but I must remind myself God has forgiven me and not wallow in self-pity because it would lead me back to the hood trying to numb the pain. I lived roasted and tortured in the fire of insanity and never want to be in such a dark and lonely place of guilt again. Each of my kids have their own horror stories and isolated events that haunt them, and it hurts me that I can't go back and change their history. Luckily, I am present *now* to make sure the good memories we are creating *today* definitely outweigh the bad ones.

Let's talk about motherly love from my mom. What can I say about Nona? Although we don't see eye to eye on everything, she is truly an amazing woman. I am blessed she has always been there for me and my three children, no matter the expense. She has spent numerous nights on the floor weeping and mourning, not knowing if I was alive or dead. She was scared every binge/mission I took I would never come home again. My mother grieved and witnessed her precious daughter slowly killing herself, only to feel HELPLESS. Nobody can "fix" an addict. The cure comes after reaching deep into our souls with all we have left and asking God or our higher power to carry us because we are too exhausted to continue life alone. Not even a wonderful mother, awesome kids, or loving spouse can compete with addiction. They will lose every time. We must fight the battle and LOVE ourselves to feel worthy of pulling up from the situation. SELF-LOVE AND EDUCATION IS THE KEY!

I was incarcerated almost two years without seeing my son and only seeing my girls two or three times. My mother refused to let Austin visit me in jail even though I wore scrubs and lived at a facility with no bars, handcuffs, or jail cells. My mom felt she was protecting him, but all she did was lie to him, and he never got to touch me, hug me, or kiss me and know I was okay. Despite the counselors telling her to bring him, she refused. I think *she* was unable to face the reality of who I had become and couldn't fathom seeing me in that environment. Honestly, I RESENT her selfishness, as I would go out of my comfort zone for my kids every time-especially if they begged me to be in court with them. However, she did what she felt was right, and I am grateful they had their Nona in their lives.

As much as I grew up blaming my mom for, I now realize I was the problem. Taking blame and being accountable was my first step toward healing. I love her and can never thank her for spending ten years of her life chasing after redeeming her daughter and bringing me home (emotionally and physically). I only wish she realized we are winners now that I am home and let go of the past. Her anger keeps her from moving forward and is robbing her of so much joy. I can't take any of it back or replace time lost, but we could have a beautiful relationship now if she would just let go and live in the present. My dear reader, that is the key here: we must realize that our addiction leaves others wounded as well. It will take TIME, PATIENCE, and WORK to rebuild a life after addiction, but there is HOPE it can happen.

Barbara, my stepmother, has also been there for me consistently. She has been on my side when others wanted to wash their hands of me. Conversely, she has also been so angry she was ready to give up on me too, but never did. Her Christian faith guided her as a role model, and I respect her values and the way she loved my father. I hurt her along the way too but was always blessed to have my family willing to accept me back every time. My dad has passed, and I miss him dearly. Daddy was always the life of the party either by playing music and singing or telling jokes. I put him through such unnecessary pain and wasted ten years I could have had with him. TIME keeps ticking on; we can't rewind the clock. TICK TOCK. He is gone now, but I am so thankful I was able to overcome and rebuild myself before he passed away. My daddy went to heaven knowing his little girl was back and found comfort in knowing I was going to be okay.

Motherly love is powerful and peaceful. I feel my kids love and respect me again and support me by standing right alongside me in this journey of speaking my truth. They have learned a few hard life lessons on our journey and are prepared for real life and all its glory. It feels good for them to call me for advice or lean on me when they are going through a rough time. I never imagined I could have this again with them, but I do. With patience, *you can too.* We must remember just because we come home from rehab or jail feeling cured, healed, and ready to forge forward, our loved ones are still stuck in our lying, manipulating, and depression. We must give them time to discover the new person we grew into. Is there a relationship you want to mend? Do you have burned bridges with someone you wish you could reunite with? IT IS POSSIBLE. I learned to C.O.P.E. and get my life back. Change requires ACTION. Are you ready to start mending your relationships?

──── CHAPTER EIGHTEEN ────

"HEY, LALA"

As I grow, develop, and progress, I realize how backward our family had become from the norm. Being I went from a "Super Mom" to a virtually absent one, I caused a shift to occur. Throughout the latter years of my addiction, my kids actually mothered me and gave me some of the wisest and most sound advice I've ever gotten. They were forced to grow up fast and in doing so, they became a wealth of knowledge and power.

Lauren filled in some of the gaps with tending to Amber and Austin when I was absent. She has a pure and loving heart of gold. Even though I had missed Lauren's previous birthday, she went out of her way to make things better for her siblings when I didn't show up on theirs. I remember my cousin, Sherr, driving to Albuquerque from Texas to visit me one summer and go with us to Amber's Regional Junior Olympic track event in Phoenix, Arizona. I had been doing well in an outpatient rehab center and was making progress learning my strengths, weaknesses, and triggers. Gene and I had a large two-story brick home, wonderful jobs, and all three children under one roof living with us. Life seemed to be turning around for me, and I could see a normal family life calling me from up ahead. Of course, my friend cocaine was jealous and demanded my attention, and for no rhyme or reason, I ran off again. I left my cousin there to take care of my household while she provided love to my heart-broken, yet angry kids.

With me being on a mission and Austin's birthday around the corner, they prepared for the worst. Sherr and my girls made Austin a lawn-mower cake and planned a party for him. Lauren and Amber wanted to make sure he was happy. Fortunately, I was able to find strength to get home the day before his party but was in no shape to bake a cake or even stay awake. I am forever thankful for my cousin and her patience with me through all the years of ups and downs. Lauren was right up front, ready to step up in my absence, and Amber was right alongside doing her part in playing with Austin and keeping him distracted from my absence.

I never sobered up long enough to realize what my kids were going through because as I started existing in real-time, I made sure to run off and numb the pain as it began to consume me. A few years later, after my divorce from Gene and a geographical move, Lauren graduated and started living a responsible life in her own house at age nineteen. She mailed me a letter when I was in prison that plunged me to my knees and slapped me across the face with her reality through my addiction. She had written her senior term paper, "Hey LaLa," and wanted to share it with me. This is how it starts:

"Hey, LaLa" was what I heard from the other side of my door as I was about to pull the trigger and take my life . . .

Apparently, Lauren had gotten Gene's revolver after school, locked herself in her room, and knelt down beside her bed to commit suicide. Austin knocked on her door saying "Hey LaLa . . . I'm hungry" and she immediately realized how much Austin and Amber needed her around.

As I'm writing this I'm drowning in tears to realize how close I came to losing my precious daughter because of my selfish binges of "fun." (Both daughters wanted to die at some point during this horrible time.) How did I not see what I was doing to them? How can we be so selfish and unaware? Addiction takes ownership of us in every aspect, and we allow things to just go by us in slow motion. What goes up must come down, and I almost lost my precious daughters along the way. They were both so tired of my disappearing acts and embarrassment that they just wanted to escape it too. I was home for weeks and months at a time in between relapses, which only left them on a roller coaster ride of emotions.

Recently, Lauren revealed this was not a true story. She admitted having times she thought she wanted to leave her life behind, so she wrote this in hopes of helping me understand. WOW. Again, my daughter was parenting me.

The summer before Amber was to start high school my dad and Barbara had come to Albuquerque to visit. I left the house to get ingredients for him to make gumbo and ran into somebody at the grocery store that triggered me and, boom—just like that, I relapsed and disappeared. Amber had given me an ultimatum and said she was giving me one year to get my life together and if I didn't, she was leaving me to go live with her dad and Lauren in Texas. I had been sober and doing well several months but was triggered instantly and within minutes had fallen again. I continued to run around high on a three-day mission while my dad had driven his RV 1,200 miles to visit me and bring me a guitar he wanted me to have. I got pulled over, went to jail for a warrant, and my Amber Bamber left me. She packed up and took off to her dad's, and I never got her back under my roof again. I tried several times to pull it together, but after returning yet again to my abuser, the domestic abuse was in full swing, and I didn't have any fight left in me. I was defeated by addiction, abuse, and myself.

Even at age six Austin was smarter than me. He said once, "Momma, can me and you go live by ourselves without Daddy? He's mean." Why can't we, as adults, see things so clearly in black and white instead of justifying with shades of gray? I should have listened and *heard* him. Jerry was in prison five years of his six-and-one-half-year life, and he had never been exposed to Jerry's angry abusive side before but witnessed an altercation that scared him, and he still holds resentment toward Jerry for the violence. Gene had always raised Austin with love, gentleness, patience, and explanations, which was far different than what he was witnessing with Jerry.

After I got home from prison all bright and shiny, Lauren and Amber were extremely supportive and continued to "mother" me. I was supposed to be the adult, yet instead my daughters were already becoming amazing pillars of strength and teaching me forgiveness through their actions. Austin displayed unconditional love for me even through his anger and confusion as well. There is light at the end of the tunnel as I am proof relationships can mend, rebuild stronger, and grow into healthy bonds. My kids all need me in their lives, and I am grateful to have lived through all my horrible choices so I can be a voice of reason on the other end of the phone for them. It feels good to be the strong adult *they* can lean on now instead of them having to carry me. The silver lining here is they are resilient kids, capable of adaptation and clear communication.

CHAPTER NINETEEN

DOING TIME, HEALING, AND SURVIVING

Doing time in a parish jail stripped me of all my vanity. Telling a Texas beauty queen she can't wear makeup, dye her hair, use a hair dryer, or paint her nails for an entire year could have been plenty punishment enough! My experiences during incarceration humbled me a great deal. It seems crazy to complain about a new facility with air conditioning, plenty of food on the trays, and an opportunity to buy chips, candy, soda, coffee, and so on at the "store." Although these things seemed a blessing, the crookedness, prejudice, and attitudes in the jail environment left me completely bitter and miserable. Women are limited to just a few outside jobs because too many end up pregnant. I literally lived in the same room for a year and watched firsthand how prejudice works and just how crooked and manipulative people can be. The favoritism creates animosity between the inmates when one goes to lockdown for something another one openly and freely gets away with. I got tired of hearing the famous saying, "Its jail, Boo!" or "Don't come to jail if you don't like it." Corruption will happen anywhere the opportunity arises.

I felt torn between my professional side where doctor's respected me for my knowledge, and then there was me with twenty-one-year old deputies looking down and judging me as an inmate who let the addiction take over my life. Why do people talk so ugly to each other? Why do we think putting other people down will somehow make us feel superior? It was frustrating being talked to like I was worthless scum. I missed the respect and how it felt to have others trust me instead of getting strip searched at 1 a.m. while waiting in the freezing snow for our turn to "squat and cough." Incarceration damn near broke me but also afforded me the opportunity to value my freedom.

My eyes were being opened to how many things in the free world I had been taking for granted. The ugly side of jail was leaving me full of resentment and anger. I can certainly see how inmates develop anti-social personality disorders from never dealing with the anger issues. For example, I wasn't even allowed to get one photocopy of my hand-written manuscript made before having to mail the original for typing. Anything could have happened to those papers, and all my work would have been lost. Those were all obstacles thrown in my way of getting my book finished, but I knew one day I would finish this book no matter what! Now, twelve years later, I have.

Healing comes by way of many different forms: crying, writing, confronting, expressing, loving, forgiving, and taking positive action. I believe what doesn't kill us makes us stronger. It was hard being confined to a small jail in the same town the accident occurred. The emotional abuse was relentless, and I constantly heard "crack head murderer," "killer," or "Don't close your eyes bitch; you might find a needle in your arm." I was horrified and scared but portrayed a façade of calmness as not to appear weak. Jail time was much harder than prison time because the anxiety awaiting sentencing coupled with no job structure and constantly changing roommates made it depressing. Although fearful of the unknown prison would bring, I couldn't wait to go (did I say that?) because I needed a change of scenery. Time in the parish jail was miserable and we hardly ever got to go outside and feel the warm sun rays on our skin or walk around. We might have gone outside once a month. Not only was all our mail gone through, but the staff and other inmates flat out stole things from us. My mom sent me a Robin Cook (favorite author) book along with some stamps. I never received it, but saw the book on the counter when I passed by going to a visit from my dad. Once again, I was under someone else's control.

Fortunately, I was sent to a minimum security prison, which was like being at a women's camp. There were rules, restrictions, and shenanigans, but I could teach GED classes, tutor, crochet and sell items during visitation, get a weed-eating job that got me outdoors around the city, and find my place in the penal pecking order. I quickly identified the crowds I didn't want to run with and eventually found other girls I thought I could relate with. Drugs are so rampant and readily accessible in jail and prison, and I wasn't about to fall into that trap again. It is easier to score dope in jail than on the streets. I knew I was never turning back to that life again and made sure not to become comfortable in my recovery in fear that would provide a small CRACK for drugs to creep back into my life.

While I was in prison, my mom served me with papers taking custody of Austin, and I was furious and blamed them for doing this "TO ME." After this time to heal, I now realize they were protecting my son from many potentially dangerous years. They dictated I couldn't see Austin if I went back to Jerry again. I would get mad before and accuse them of trying to CONTROL my life by dictating who I could be with. I mean, it's not like I was fifteen anymore, but I've come to realize I hadn't been acting forty years old either. I was making poor choices.

The custody papers shocked me with such an enormous jolt straight to my heart and woke me up to the reality of my abusive marriage. They knew the power and control he had over me, and although they knew they couldn't keep me from returning, they *could* protect Austin. My anger about the custody has turned into gratitude they love Austin so much and my son is blessed to have their love. I am too.

I was served the custody papers on December 18, 2007 without any warning. Suddenly I realized why my mother sounded so sick, down, and tearful on her birthday December 11; it was the day she signed the papers! My poor mother spent her birthday taking custody of her treasured sunshine girl's son.

My mom is ashamed of me, although she doesn't even realize it herself. She still lives in a pretend world and *refuses* to tell some people the truth about where I was those two years. I want so badly for her to realize she is imprisoning herself by living in denial. Everything I've been through makes me WHO I AM, and although she chooses to ignore that, I love her and know she is just coping the best way she knows how. Mom, this isn't your fault. You have always been awesome. I was the failure.

She didn't let me see Austin for two years and says it was to protect him. Apparently, according to her, his doctor and Dr. Phil's TV program agreed. Well, I'm his mother and wanted to explain to my eight-year-old son who thought I was in a hospital getting better from my wreck, that I *can't* come home, not that I *won't*! To a small child, there is a big difference. I never wanted to lie to him and warned my mom Austin would be angry if she lied to him when he learned the truth. I believe in telling the truth and being accountable for our actions. Mom thought because she would be the one dealing with his anger, it was best not to tell him the truth. But if she had let him visit me for one hour every two weeks, put his arms around me, kiss me, feel me, then he would know I was okay and gain comfort in security knowing I *was* coming home again one day. I think he would have coped better than being lied to and just not seeing me at all. I still battle harboring anger over this issue and pray every day for some relief in this situation. I know my mom felt she was protecting him, but I think in reality it allowed a continuing façade to prevent her from facing the reality of it all herself.

During healing time in jail, I also endured many emotional pangs. Having to endure being in a room of glares, stares, remarks, threats, and animosity was one thing, but to do time with the two girls that assaulted me was a mind "screw." They were picked up on old warrants of prostitution, so when I arrived from the hospital, they were already in general population. I was terrified and unsure how those two girls were going to react. The last time I had seen them, one punched me in the face, and the other threw a brick at my car. Someone died, but I was the only one being charged, even though I had three eyewitnesses that saw the assault.

My first instinct was to just go off on them because they caused me to kill someone! Mentally, it was challenging to sit by them to eat and have to sleep in the same area. The tension sored after a few days, the warden noted the hostility among the pod and moved *me* into isolation.

Why me? So much favoritism goes on in jails. Girls can be a "problem" by acting up, and they get released faster. Sometimes they actually reward bad behavior! I requested to be housed in another facility to avoid further confrontations, but again, the answer was NO! It was just more small-town podunk political junk! After a few days, I was forced to return to population and just stayed on guard, always having to watch my back because every woman that came in was a potential threat as I heard her friends and family were "coming for me."

Didn't the people in the town *know* it was an accident? I was assaulted; why were they coming for me? Of course, the jail offered little protection, and several relatives ended up being allowed in population with me anyway. Get this. Two of the relatives were put in *my* cell. Go figure! Emotional stress was peaking, but I am a survivor. God had my back, *always*!

I constantly reminded myself of my sisters words, "Everything is going wrong just right because God is in control." I gained strength and learned how to forgive others. I know in order for God to forgive me, I must genuinely forgive others. This was hard because I felt it unfair I was the only one charged and the only one left to carry the burden of her death. I was the one doing time away from my family because of it. Guess where those two ended up? You got it—they returned to walking the streets, prostituting, robbing, and getting high. One of them returned in and out on new armed robbery charges and was caught up in her addictions. After she came to me crying about the wreck and blaming herself, we began to talk, and I read the Bible with her and helped her get her GED. I decided to just let God be their judge and deal with them in His time and in His way. I actually felt sympathy for both of them because they are a product of their environmental upbringing. My family is supportive and understanding and provided a stable, safe place for me, yet I still battled addiction. I couldn't imagine being alone without a place to go where drugs aren't part of everyday life or dealing with multiple addictions. I can barely handle one cocaine addiction.

I prayed they face themselves in the mirror and wake up one day with God's strength to take a stand against drugs and violence. We should drop to our knees for God, not to make money for dope. I'm sure some are saying, "I'd kick those bitch's asses," and I wanted to, but where would that get me? It won't bring her back to life, so I let go and let God. Sadly, I learned a few years ago that the one that was remorseful had overdosed and died. She was a product of her environment and upbringing and never really stood a chance at a normal life. The other twit never showed remorse, and I have no idea where she is.

The first Christmas holiday of incarceration left me extremely depressed because I cried to be with my children yet realized the lady I killed had children crying for her too. I was grieving and needed professional help in coping with all of this. I requested counseling or a mental health appointment to get back on my Lexapro for depression. I wasn't suicidal, but felt guilty I lived and she didn't. It took seven months and my dad calling the sheriff to finally get the assistant warden to make my mental health appointment.

I was treated differently by many in that town and knew they all judged me for killing her. I was allowed to drown in tears, anger, and depression without any compassion from them to get me some counseling—that was so wrong.   But again, I SURVIVED. I have created a hard shell through perseverance, but when in bed at night, my soft fragile inside still wept. The prison offered no help either. They took me off my Wellbutrin immediately when I got there. To have any job (non-paying) such as working in the yard, kitchen or library, you must not be on any psychotropic meds. I felt the depression really settling in on me, and of course food was there to comfort me. Overeating is another addiction, and those obsessive behaviors must be dealt with, or we just keep bouncing around replacing one addiction for another. I hated the time in jail and prison but am thankful for it as I understand the need for me to be accountable for my actions and pay my debt to society by doing the time for the crimes.

—— CHAPTER TWENTY ——

CONFRONTING AND REBUILDING

L iving a life of always trying to please others, becoming what they expect, being pretty enough, skinny enough, smart enough, fun enough, sensitive enough, or all-around good enough has been a tall order to try and fill. I realize most of these pressures and expectations were self-inflicted, and I am my own worst critic, wallowing in a pool of shame and inadequacy. Most of my drug usage was fueled by guilt, shame, and blame. Those powerful emotions when not dealt with were ammunition to my repeated downfall. Satan used flashbacks, bad memories, or feelings of guilt to taunt me and lure me into the temptation of letting dope numb the pain. I have had a life chock-full of guilt and manipulation. When I failed to meet expectations, others used guilt to scold me. Out of anger, my parents would throw in my face how they bailed me out financially over and over again, how co-signing for me ruined their credit, or how I wasn't there when my baby boy took his first steps. I remember guilt being used as manipulation even before I became an addict.

People close to us tend to internalize our situation and shape it into what it has done to them in their lives. When I became pregnant out of wedlock, my mom threatened not to come to the wedding and said I couldn't wear a white dress. It wasn't even *her* decision. Why did she do this? Better yet, why did I *allow* her to? I never learned to set up healthy boundaries with my loved ones and always allowed them to guilt me over and over again. When I tried to get my mom to bring Austin to visit me or come to my court hearings, she cried, "Why are you doing this to me?" and "I just can't face seeing you in handcuffs." What about me? He is my son, and it should have been my decision. I needed my family; I struggled every day just to live through my shame and guilt. Sobriety is like slamming the brakes on in our car-everything from behind us comes crashing into us in the front seat. By immediately taking accountability, we remove some of the ammo.

Attacks come in other ways too, such as Jerry throwing Scripture at me to control me. He preached against premarital sex to pressure me into marriage, preached about adultery (when he was secretly cheating on me repeatedly), or preached against divorce when I wanted to leave him. Where was the Scripture to support him picking up whores or asking me to lie in a court of law and take charges for him? Funny, he never could locate those Scriptures. Beware, the devil comes in all forms. Even though I had acquired three college degrees, gave birth to three beautiful children, and had a compassionate heart, I *allowed* him to make me feel worthless, selfish and useless.

As previously mentioned, there are one thousand regrets that can't be rewound, but if I don't let them go, I will never heal. My parents rescued me time and time again and never once said "no" when I called for help. I'm very grateful for all of their financial, physical, and emotional help, and if I could take some of their pain and anger away, I would. They have all taken turns packing and moving me out of homes while I was incarcerated. They rescued me repeatedly, and although consumed with anger, they always accepted me back. My kids have loved me uncondi-tionally. They have been angry, scared, deserted, and lied to but knew their mommy was still somewhere hidden in the shell of a body I walked around in.

I have learned to understand their anger, sympathize with their pain, and acknowledge how I hurt them and affected their lives. I am what I am today and others are who they are because of the sequences of events and influences in our lives. What good is being ashamed and feeling guilty? I am learning to forgive myself and accept my past is already written. The silver lining is I am in control of my future and have power to navigate my own journey, just as you do. Respect your moments of choice because they become your lifetime of decisions.

Today I declare to be driven under positive influences and build from my past mistakes and experiences. Although I am responsible for taking the life of another while driving under the influence, her memorial will drive me to make a difference and pave a better path for others. I pray you find your way and drive under influences of joy, peace, happiness, love, respect, success, compassion, and just simply deny the "junk in your trunk." Find comfort in Jeremiah 29:11: "For I know the future I have planned for you. It is of good, not evil. Have faith in me and I'll show you the way." Utilize the "been there, done that" attitude, keep the faith, and learn to love yourself and see your blessings.

— CHAPTER TWENTY-ONE —

COMMON DENOMINATOR

Who defines failure for us? What defines it for us? Do you internalize everything that isn't just perfect in your life as *your* failure? Have you blamed yourself for a failed marriage or for not getting a promotion at work even when you performed your best and deserved it? Have you ever blamed yourself for your child becoming addicted to drugs? I still battle the noose of depression when I feel a sense of failure. Failed marriages, failed parenting, failed attempts to be stronger than cocaine, failed weight loss, failed career goals, and failed self-forgiveness all contribute to depression, but we should not allow it to consume us. My perfectionism leaves me expecting so much from those around me. I place such high expectations, people are sure to fail me, then I internalize and assume it was my fault when they don't measure up. This viscous cycle must be broken if we want to take our lives to the next level. We must take culpability for our part, but only our part. Hold others accountable for their part and let them carry their own emotional baggage.

Words hurt! Failure hurts! Life hurts! My previous marriages failed for one reason or another, and I've been told it must be me because I'm the common denominator. Until now, I've always disagreed because I didn't

131

force them to cheat, court their porn addiction, drink behind my back, lie, or hit me. But here is a truth bomb: it *is* me! Currently going through a divorce from Neil, I've given this much thought and practiced what I preach to search for the positive in each situation. I truly believe I have found the problem. I'm the one choosing partners that hurt me. Instead of getting upset, insecure, resentful, and hurt over them replacing our sex life with their own personal porn relationship, lying about drinking, leaving me for my roommate in rehab, or getting another woman pregnant, I ask myself, "Is this the type of man I want to be with?" Instead of ridiculing them for their choices and trying to change them, I need to focus on me and my bad choice in choosing them as a mate. Unfortunately, most major issues are hidden behind elaborate lies, and we don't find out until we have years invested in the relationship. Is it really too much to ask for honesty, loyalty, and respect from a mate? I can offer those things; why can't I receive them? Do you find yourself asking these same questions? I know I'm not alone in this tangled web of deception. I'd love to know how some can stay in a marriage where trust, respect, and honesty have been lost. Counseling doesn't help when your partner lives so embedded in their own lies they lie to the counselor! Do these relationships truly heal, or do people put their happiness on a shelf and "pretend" they have it all? It seems I've been married to the same man, just with four different names. I don't want to fake it until I make it; I want true happiness! Don't you? Don't we deserve it?

If you find yourself up the same tortuous creek without a paddle, we have to raise our water level to attract those healthier fish. As we grow, become true to ourselves, identify our inner pain, and heal, our water level rises. With higher water levels, we will attract other healthy mates who have gone through the same low tide drought. If you are ready to rise and go after what you know you deserve, join me in learning to embrace personal faults and assuming accountability. We must ACT to get a reAC-Tion. We must take the first bold step toward healing by identifying our faults and shortcomings, clearly learning how to be an effective communicator, and looking through positive filters instead of negative ones. There is more than one way to skin a cat, so we must train our brain to see both sides of the coin and not immediately jump to "it must be my fault" or "it is all their fault." As our journey to find ourselves comes to fruition, we can identify things to love about ourselves, and from there we build a new and improved foundation with stronger building blocks. With our new knowledge to pick and choose our battles and live a simpler life without blame-shifting and expectations, we will start to be ourselves, we will be *more* than we were before. It is unrealistic to think others will never hurt us; therefore, we must quit expecting perfection. We must come to terms with realizing everyone thinks differently, and our way isn't the only way. Always being right and staying closeminded to only one side of the coin will just keep us miserable and feeling inadequate. With my four step C.O.P.E. method we start pulling ourselves up because we learn to become accountable for our own faults. However, we must realize everything isn't our fault just because things didn't fit our plan. Look up, step up, get up, and pull yourself up! Utilize my C.O.P.E. system to begin your new journey.

CHAPTER TWENTY-TWO

MOVING FORWARD

I have learned not to let someone else's words or LACK of words determine my happiness. Codependency is harmful and robs us of our own identity and independence. We should edify each other and attract "pretty" fish in our ocean. I've witnessed firsthand the domestic violence cycle I once said I'd never put up with. I was conned and charmed every time into BELIEVING he was sorry or he had changed. Don't fall for that! They rarely truly change. Again, don't take my word for it but look up the statistics: the twenty phone calls every day weren't really because he missed me, but to "track" me. He had even convinced me my black eyes were prompted by *my* smart mouth or overly flirtatious ways. Boy, was I a fool! Why does it take us so long to see the manipulations our loved ones see so plainly in black and white?

I have shared clues, insights, and wisdom on what to do if you find yourself in a situation you know isn't good for you. EVERY decision we make in life is date and time stamped, but so is the action in motion for the recovery period. By allowing time to heal individual wounds, I've learned a great deal about myself. I was lonely and desperate to be loved and ACCEPTED by any man. I now rely on myself for happiness and have stopped shifting blame on others for my unhappiness. Remember, the vibes we put out will attract the same vibes on the same frequency. We need to resonate a healthier vibe.

"Sharing is caring" and "giving is receiving." I dare you to actually practice these simple sayings and still feel the world has crashed down on you or failed you. If focused on others, we won't dwell on our problems and hide behind depression. I finally own my stuff—good and bad! I am seeking my purpose, living life shame free, and feeling such freedom and relief. It isn't all roses and cupcakes every day, but I learned to utilize necessary tools to get me through the bad days. Additionally, I focus on giving back and helping others, and my life becomes less dramatic and chaotic when I do. I am ready to shout the secrets I've spent so many years protecting. NO MORE line dancing with shame, blame, and guilt crowding me. Once I learned it isn't about me anymore, I gained courage, strength, and motivation to use what happened to me to help others by letting it flow through me. It already happened to me, and I survived, so now I am ready to confront, challenge, change, and conquer the world with powerful, positive, and meaningful insight, hoping to make an IMPACT on others.

Do you have a story inside weighing you down keeping you at the bottom of the ocean? Let it flow out of you and dance around on paper or in the air as you tell somebody. Just dig it out of you with honesty and watch your life change. Feel the transition as you raise your water level and confront your demons with determination and triumph. Do you want to live? Do you want to get out of the rut you have fallen in? There is hope! Confront, Optimize, Push through, and Embrace to become a better you.

FIND yourself, LOVE yourself, BE yourself. . . . PULL YOURSELF UP!

Slow down, enjoy the journey and use the clutch! If you get there too fast, you won't be ready. Learn patience, be forgiving and find your purpose. Respect your moment of choice by taking a little longer to make a decision by first thinking it through to the end. Choices will determine your legacy. And finally, stop hiding! George Bernard Shaw said it best: "If you can't get rid of the skeletons in your closet, then you better teach them to dance." I'm ready to dance, are you?

Dear Reader, I want so badly for you to make a connection and feel you have gained something from my story. Your journey is sure to be one of emotion, betrayal, and some level of denial. I pray you take the time you deserve to sort it out, write it down, or share with someone all that haunts you. Now that you have been given my four step C.O.P.E.=HOPE method to start healing, I challenge you to engage in the process. I would absolutely love to hear from you about your thoughts, suggestions, or success stories from using the C.O.P.E. = HOPE method. I have been transparent in hopes of liberating you to do the same so you can witness the freedom it brings. We are all in this world together, and I am your sister for life. Please reach out to me whenever you feel compelled. Feel free to email me directly from my website at www.mistielayne.com , reach out on any social media platform (mistie layne), or direct message me. I want to be the person you can relate to and UNDERSTANDS you because I've lived it. I also want to be the person who doesn't *allow* you to make excuses or procrastinate (because I've been there too.) TOGETHER we can start a movement. Let's strive to JUDGE less and MENTOR more to IMPACT the world with compassion, education, and honesty. I love you and thank you for coming into my life. GO BE YOUR BEAUTIFUL SELF. PULL YOURSELF UP!

Please remember, if you don't like the way your story is going, write a different ending. You ARE in control now. BE BRAVE and help ease suffering of others.

Love,

Mistie Layne

Miss Sabine River Racer, 8th grade with mom and dad.

Tap solo recital pic 1980

POEMS FROM PRISON

"Paying the price" with heart, body and soul

NEGLIGENT
HOMICIDE
(A HAIKU)

She's gone, I'm to blame
Left behind to feel the pain
Forgiveness I pray

Head twirler, Homecoming 1984

MDC mugshot 2002

"Changes"   by Mistie 2/6/08

One unfortunate morning,
  my life changed without warning

I had been struggling with Satan
  and been upset and hating

I lost sight of my Lord
  but got cut down by Satan's sword

Quickly, I fell into that trap again
  and I was wrong, I won't pretend

I took the life of another
  Can I forgive myself, I wonder?

I know our pain isn't the same
  but I hurt and carry the guilt and blame

It was an accident you see
  I wish you only knew me

I'm full of respect, passion, and love
  I worship my Savior from above

I was living my life to serve Him
  then my husband's fist made my life grim

I was in a place I shouldn't have been
unfortunate events happened, then her life came to an
                                             end.

page 2

If I could turn back the clock I would
~~I'm~~ asking your forgiveness if you could?

My life has since changed, your's too
mine has been saved, while your's is bleu

My heart aches with your pain
if only the truth you could gain

I hope ~~Desiree~~ she is looking down on me
and will be my angel and not flee

I need her to guide my life
her death removed me from strife

I promise her dying was not just your loss
my heart stays trampled and tossed.

I vow to live for her out there
to pave a better road and prepare

With God I know she rests
and may your family He bless

As for me, I wanted to die too
but now I want to live for me and you!

I thank God for sparing my life that day
And for your daughter's death, forgiveness I pray.

                    God Bless Your Family,
                         mistie

Turmoil & Chaos

Mistie 1-24-08

Still confined and lonely among twenty girls
but not the kind that wear Gucci and pearls

Surrounded by gossip, lies and manipulation
ten months of it have caused frustration

This cell is constantly closing in on me
Green walls and floors is all I ever see

Ten steps to the shower, five to the phone,
No wonder I'm losing muscle tone!

Writing a book about my life
depression cutting me like a knife

Desperate to get a message out there
DRUGS TAKE LIVES, please BEWARE

I regret the time wasted on cocaine
destructive memories haunt me and drive me insane

Shame and guilt spun cobwebs in my head
praying for peace and forgiveness instead

I miss my children so very much,
my body aches just for their touch

haunted by a tragic death I caused last year
    my life is on the line — now I fear

Grief and sorrow I'm burdened to carry every day
    scared of the consequences I'm sentenced to pay

I cry to return to my "NORMAL" life
    before cocaine caused havoc and strife

Inner growth was accomplished this year
    I can finally move forward without fear

My emotions roll around like fog, then fade
    my life became train wrecked as satan played

So ready to surrender my life to God
    I learned to "FEAR" him while locked in this pod

So much to say but my words seem cluttered
    they are dying to be HEARD, not just muttered

I'm anxious to spread my testimony around
    to preach of a new way of life I've found

To love myself and find inner peace
    I tore up my contract with satan's lease

Praying for release from my own bondage
    Now to my Lord and Savior I pay hommage

Lost and tossed are my thoughts, feelings + heart
a life with focus, peace and clarity to start

Lord hear my plea as my heart drips blood
Save me fast before I drown in this flood

I NEED all my racing thoughts to slow down
I want a smile of calmness to evolve from my
frown

All in all, am I asking for too much?
God, I beg you ... reach me with your
healing touch!

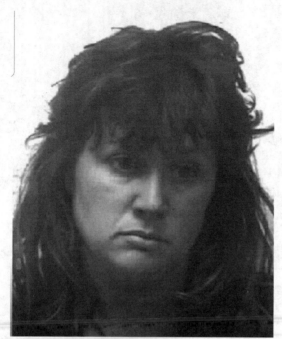

MDC mugshot 2003

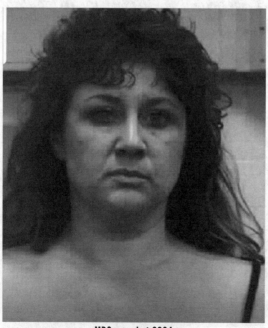

MDC mugshot 2004

"Troubled Soul"
by Mistie

8/7/08

Misery and despair all in the air
emotions spinning and tossing like cyclones

Sadness and sorrow of yesterdays regrets
come and go like the seasons rotate

Pain and grief consume my thoughts
anxiety and disassociation are evident

The facade of happiness, I carry well
but inside feeling pulled in shreds

My mind is racing with thoughts and memories
constantly trying to condem my soul

I try and block satan's strategic moves
but end up ~~tied~~ tangled in insanity

Sometimes I feel a part of me is dead
but sometimes wish all of me were numb.

Never to take my own life though —
I'm my worst critic, punishing myself
to ease the pain from webs of guilt

②

Serenity is a beautiful word by definition
  but its meaning has never made
    the reality connection in _my_ world!

Lies, lies, full of false hapiness
  searching for a place ju_st_ _to_ belong
    where others understand my song

Too busy being a people pleaser
  that I rebelled, rebuked and lost
  my independency and idenity

Does anyone _EVER_ know who they are?
  do they look in the mirror and actually
  find solace in _THAT_ person?

Criticism, guilt, shame, and pain
  that is the treacherous zone I'm stuck
  in sucking me in like quick-sand.

Surrounded by life lines and the love of my family
  because I'm scared that has vanished
      from my painful soul

③

Hoping, wishing, praying to resurrect
the innocence I lost long ago,
yet another disappointment

Desperate to find my own way to become
meaningful space instead of settled dust
removing the luster of what it touches

Looking for a way out of this tainted body + soul
dreaming of some kind of reincarnation

Inside my head lies a labyrinth of nightmares
memories and now sorrow

These thoughts racing tirelessly thru my mind
not a single moment of peace can I find?

Does the lonliness ever go away
or is doom and gloom here to stay?

I've realized there is nobody to rescue me
the strength must come from within— NOW I SEE
I MUST get up and fight the depression + cravings back
I must use my words to fight against Crack.

Author headshot 2019

— PAIN I'VE CAUSED —

(to my parents)
Mistie Layne

My drug addiction has not only affected my life, but has greatly impacted yours too. I know first and foremost you are heartbroken that I turned out the way I have. I'm sure you try and blame yourself but you raised me with good values and morals and it was my own failures in life that led me to go down that dark and lonely path. Please don't blame yourself.

I have also hurt you financially and I want to pay you back even though all you ever say is you just want Mistie Layne back. I've betrayed your trust, lied to you and manipulated you repeatedly and am so sorry for all of that. I know it hurts you to see the sadness and emptiness in my eyes and you wonder where your little girl went. I'm in here, somewhere. I'm still fighting to win this battle and want to climb out of this hell but every time I try, I fail. I'm so sorry. I promise I will keep trying. I miss my family so much.

I hate robbing you of memories we should have built the last ten years together. My fear is you will die before I find my way HOME. You have driven mile after mile "hunting" me down while I was missing and sacrificed so many things for me and my children. I know my actions are selfish and I truly want to stop this madness….HELP ME. What can I do? I promise you, I HAVE TRIED. I really have…. Everytime I think I'm free from it, I fall again. This is so hard. How can I say I love my kids yet choose to run off for days at a time? You can't understand, nobody can.

I am living in my own HELL. How did I ever get this way? Somebody please save me. I just want to be ME again. I have the DESIRE, just can't muster the STRENGTH. The cravings are so intense and honestly I just want the shame and guilt to go away so relapsing "feels" therapeutic. I know this is silly and makes no sense to you, but to anyone under this bondage, it is real.

I'm sorry I'm no longer your sunshine girl momma. I am so dark and ugly, inside and out now. The things I've done and witnessed have forever tarnished my soul. I am no longer bright and shiny.

I'm sorry daddy. I know I was destined to be better and yall gave me every chance in life to succeed. I did this, not you. If you don't give up on me, I promise I won't give up on me either.

Love,
Mistie

—13ᵀᴴ ROUND EXHAUSTION—

Mistie Layne

I'm exhausted like I'm in the 13th round of a boxing match where my ass got whipped, punked, beat up, humiliated and lost my ranking. My body felt so worn after coming off a six day crack mission, with little to no sleep. The morning of September 18, 2007, I had been high 24/7 and my body was barely functioning. My make-up was smeared from 2 days before and my eyes were in the "greenish blue" phase of my last beating. I was falling asleep before the devil's candy even melted on my pipe for me to smoke it. My eyelids barely opened after closing to blink and I NEEDED the cocaine to stay awake and find a safe place to sleep until I mustered the strength to face my family and return home.

I knew I was "out there" this time and pushed myself physically further than ever before. I was in agony and completely CONSUMED by shame and guilt. I desperately wanted deep down inside my HELL-BOUND soul to be arrested, killed or MIRACULOUSLY delivered from craving hit after hit after hit. I wanted to stop the madness so badly, but needed to be high to survive. I was too tired to pee, eat, think, or even breathe sometimes.

My missions always started out like a boxing match where you are light on your feet, full of energy and vigor. At the beginning of a mission I could think, move around, and strategize. But just like a boxing match, after a few rounds we grow weary, our vision is blurred, and our feet become heavy as if wearing those steel boots to walk under water in. The recovery period was brief (like between boxing rounds) but I gained motivation to conquer my addiction and tackled it head on, only to walk back into the rink to get knocked right back down with deeper cuts and less drive. Too tired to get back up and even conquer breathing. If breathing wasn't an involuntary reflex, I would be dead for sure. My mouth would be so cut up I didn't want to even crack (pun) my lips open.. but knew I had to in order to inhale the cursed smoke into my lungs.

I was ready to give up, no longer holding any hope I could ever overcome this bondage. But, I never once said.."I'm going to kill someone today." I gave the girls a ride and just needed to get high to stay awake. They attacked me, punched me in my already bruised face, broke my glasses and I panicked. I turned the car around to get the hell out of there and they threw a brick at me and I swerved and lost control of my car.... Then, IT happened and it was permanent. After coming to and having a couple of days to sleep and regain consciousness, my heart bleeds like a butchered animal and the pain is unbearable. My altered brain refuses to believe this is real life... it has to be a dream. God, please say this is a dream and I didn't really kill that lady. What is going to happen to me now? Is it fair I am even alive? My poor kids. I was such a good mommy.....Mistie....where are you??? How can you do this to your wonderful kids? Who am I?

My mind is a continuous waterfall of blame and remorse and I'm stuck at the bottom constantly being shoved underwater suffocating. I'm so tired, simply exhausted! Is the fight over yet? Surely, I've lost. I'm throwing in the towel, I can't box another round. Mistie is long gone and I'm too exhausted to look for her.

— BITING MY TONGUE —

Mistie Layne

THEN

When my very abusive and psycho husband held me hostage over insane jealousy, I had to bite my tongue in fear he would literally go into a rage and kill me. When he slipped into his rages, he spiraled out of control with wild accusations and far-fetched ideals. I HATED holding my tongue because I wanted to tell him I hated every single fiber in his body and how I dreamt of breaking all 206 of his bones. I visualized taking a sledge hammer and smashing him in the mouth so he could just once feel the pain he routinely inflicted upon me. I had to MUTE my anger in fear of his physical consequences. Being in an abusive relationship really had me timid, meek and without identity. This was not at all the Mistie everyone knew. THAT girl was long gone with little hope of ever coming back.

He used every insecurity I had and expounded on it as leverage to CONTROL me. He used my weight to put me down, yet got mad if anyone gave me attention. He would tell me I was beautiful one day, then the next I was a fat whore!!! He kept me spinning and bouncing around in my own head constantly. I had to wear shirts under my scrubs in fear somebody might "see" down my shirt if I bent over and leaned over at 30 degrees just right. Ha! Why did he care? I thought I was just a fat whore anyway? And, why did he marry me if he thought so little of me? If the phone rang without anyone on the other end, I got a beating for it because

155

it was sure to be somebody I was screwing. He assumed when I opened the mini blinds above the kitchen sink that it was a sign for the neighbor to "come and get it." The cocaine completely warped his brain and caused so much paranoia. Sex was on HIS TERMS and ONLY his terms. If I tried to dress in lingerie to spark his interest, he would say….what is that suppose to do for me?...look at you! Then, the next day he brought me roses and told me how beautiful I was and couldn't get enough of me. Is this regular domestic abuse or is he truly a psychopath with a split personality… I mean, who can keep up?

He would scold me in public to the point I wanted to hide behind a bush, a car, anything!!! Very rarely would anyone dare interfere and try and help me. I remember in grade school being taught if I was ever being raped to yell FIRE, not RAPE because people don't want to get involved. This is sad and just pisses me off. He would come sit at the hospital to check up on me and make sure I was actually working and checked my phone, pager and voice mails constantly. Once I had to go and hang films in the radiologist reading rooms for the on-call doctor to read the procedure I had just performed. The doctor and I had a discussion about the patient and his scan and it took a few minutes longer than usual for me to come out. Radiology reading rooms are dark so the films can be seen and he assumed I was in there screwing the guy (while he stood outside the door.) Seriously? That night was one of the worst beatings he gave me. All I could remember caring about was me praying I didn't get called back into the hospital that night because my eyes were black and swollen almost shut, my nose was busted and my lips were swollen. I looked like a blow fish.

I HATE HIM. I HATE HIM. I HATE HIM.

— BITING MY TONGUE —

(Continued)

NOW

Looking back after being out from under his control for 12 years now, I wonder HOW I ever allowed all of this to happen. I know he used cocaine to keep me where he wanted me, but even during the clean times between relapses, he controlled me. I finally became wise to his "honeymoon" phase apologies and the mentally abusive cycle he created. *He changed me.* For a while, I became lifeless, hopeless and fightless…

Then, after jail forced a physical separation, I began to see a little more clearly. The real ME showed up. The ME buried under the fear, shame and insecurity. I showed up ready to emerge and take control of MY LIFE. I worked hard to find my inner strengths and gifts. I looked in the mirror every day and found just one thing positive to say about myself and said it all day long. The more focus I put on liking, then loving myself, the stronger I grew. Prison put the physical separation between us, but I MADE the break from him emotionally all on my own. I learned I didn't love myself and therefore didn't feel worthy of anyone else's love either. Once I started finding things to love about me, I realized I was worthy and just because I had made a mess of my life, my life wasn't over. My MESS would serve as a MESSAGE for you to find yourself, love yourself and be yourself. Now is the time to PULL YOURSELF UP!

Although BITING MY TONGUE was hard with the volatile storm of anger raging inside me, I am thankful I did because it kept me alive. Yes, *HE CHANGED ME*. He created this powerful, experienced, driven woman full of love, passion and insight. He gave me the determination to FIGHT. Now, I want to fight for other women still stuck biting their tongues and tell them THERE IS HOPE. We can thrive without them and WE CAN repair the damage and move forward. The emotional and physical scars may not ever go away, but they are badges of honor that we were NOT DEFEATED!!!!! We lived. We evolved. We grew into our places and NOW we must grow into our destiny as well.

Thank you abusive husband, *YOU CHANGED ME!!!!!*